My poor dad often said, "What you know is important." My rich dad said, "If you want to be rich, <u>who</u> you know is more important than <u>what</u> you know."

Rich Dad explained further saying, "Business and investing are team sports." The average investor or small-business person loses financially because they do not have a team. Instead of a team, they act as individuals who are trampled by very smart teams.

That is why the Rich Dad's Advisors book series was created. Rich Dad's Advisors will offer guidance to help you know who to look for and what kind of questions to ask so you can gather your own great team of advisors.

Other Bestselling Books
by Robert T. Kiyosaki with Sharon L. Lechter

Rich Dad Poor Dad
What The Rich Teach Their Kids About Money—
That The Poor And Middle Class Do Not!

Rich Dad's CASHFLOW Quadrant
Rich Dad's Guide To Financial Freedom

Rich Dad's Guide to Investing
What The Rich Invest In, That The
Poor and Middle Class Do Not!

Rich Dad's Rich Kid Smart Kid
Give Your Child A Financial Head Start

Rich Dad's Retire Young Retire Rich
How To Get Rich Quickly And Stay Rich Forever

Rich Dad's Prophecy
Why The Biggest Stock Market Crash In History Is Still Coming...
And How You Can Prepare Yourself And Profit From It!

Rich Dad's Success Stories
Real Life Success Stories from Real Life People
Who Followed the Rich Dad Lessons

Rich Dad's Guide To Becoming Rich
Without Cutting Up Your Credit Cards
Turn "Bad Debt" into "Good Debt"

Rich Dad's Who Took My Money?
Why Slow Investors Lose and Fast Money Wins!

Rich Dad Poor Dad for Teens
The Secrets About Money—
That You Don't Learn in School!

Rich Dad's ADVISORS

The ABC's of Getting Out of Debt

Turn Bad Debt Into Good Debt and Bad Credit Into Good Credit

Garrett Sutton, Esq.

WARNER
BUSINESS
BOOKS™

NEW YORK   BOSTON

Copyright © 2004 by Garrett Sutton, Esq.
All rights reserved.

Published by Warner Books in association with CASHFLOW® Technologies, Inc., and BI Capital Inc.

CASHFLOW, Rich Dad, Rich Dad's Advisors, Rich Dad's Seminars, the BI Triangle, and CASHFLOW Quadrant (ESBI Symbol) are registered trademarks of CASHFLOW® Technologies, Inc. Rich Kid Smart Kid, Rich Dad Australia, Rich Dad's Coaching, and Journey to Financial Freedom are trademarks of CASHFLOW® Technologies, Inc.

   are registered trademarks of CASHFLOW® Technologies, Inc.

Visit our Web site at www.richdad.com

Success DNA and Altacian Corporate Services, Inc. are registered trademarks of Success DNA, Inc. Sutton Law Center is a registered trademark of Sutton Law Center PC.

Warner Business Books

Time Warner Book Group, 1271 Avenue of the Americas, New York, NY 10020.
Visit our Web site at: www.twbookmark.com.

The Warner Business Books logo is a trademark of Warner Books.

Printed in the United States of America

First Printing: November 2004
10 9 8 7 6 5

Library of Congress Cataloging-in-Publication Data
Sutton, Garrett.
    The ABC's of getting out of debt : turn bad debt into good debt and bad credit into good credit / Garrett Sutton.
        p.   cm.—(Rich dad's advisors)
    ISBN 0-446-69409-6
    1. Finance, Personal.   2. Consumer credit.   3. Debt.   I. Title.   II. Rich dad's advisors series.

HG179.S877   2004
338.024'02—dc22

2004017353

Acknowledgments

The author would like to acknowledge the invaluable contributions of several individuals in the preparation of this book. First, I am indebted to Gerri Detweiler, America's premier expert on credit and debt issues, for her keen insights and advice on the overall drafting of this book. Second, Dr. Kenji Sax was very helpful in formulating the psychology of debt section. I must also thank Brian Sandoval, Nevada's attorney general, and his deputies, Jo Ann Gibbs and Neil Rombardo, for their assistance in identifying the numerous credit scams that exist in the marketplace. Robert and Kim Kiyosaki are sincerely acknowledged for providing the story of their own personal debt reduction plan and experience. A tip of the hat is due to Dan Ambrosio and Robert Castillo of Warner Books and Sharon Lechter of the Rich Dad Company for their excellent efforts in keeping the process on track. My staff, as always, has been very helpful, especially Kristy Muck, Canyon Cassidy, and Matthew Dearing in the Reno office. And finally, another thankful acknowledgment for their patience as this book was being written is due to my wife, Jenny; and children, Teddy, Emily, and Sarah.

Contents

I Love My Credit Cards

In the late 1980s, I went to a seminar on financial success. The instructor, a young charismatic speaker, went on and on about the perils of debt, saying repeatedly, "Debt is bad. Debt is your enemy. Get out of debt as soon as you can." Looking around the room at approximately fifty attendees, I could see most heads were nodding in agreement.

Just before the break, the young speaker asked, "Okay, are you ready to cut your ties with the bondage of debt?" Most attendees nodded. "If you are ready to break the bonds, then stand, get out your credit cards, and hold them up high so everyone in the room can see them." Most of the class stood immediately while there were several people, like me, who were looking around waiting to see if we should follow or not. Slowly, everyone stood, myself included. I figured that since I had paid money and invested this much time, I might as well go along with the process to see what I could learn. As I held my gold credit card in front of me, a smiling assistant handed me a pair of scissors. As I grasped the scissors, I knew what was to happen next. "Okay, class, cut your credit cards in half," said the instructor. As I heard the sounds of scissors cutting through plastic, there were actually several cries of shock, some groans, and even a few people crying. After cutting my card in half, I just stood in silence, mostly numb, waiting for some form of educated enlightenment to sweep over me. Nothing happened. I just felt numb. Although I had been in credit card trouble in the late 1970s, when my nylon and Velcro wallet business was caving in on me, I did eventually clean up my debt and had gone on to use my credit cards more responsibly; hence I did not have the same cathartic reaction some people in the class seemed to have when they cut their cards in half.

In less than a week, my replacement card had arrived in the mail and I was happily on my way, using my gold card again. Although I did not have a blinding cognition after cutting my credit card, the process did make me more aware of how much of a problem credit, primarily its use and abuse, can be in a person's life. Today I watch many so-called financial experts saying the same things that young instructor was saying years ago, such things as "Get out of debt." "Cut up your credit cards." "Put your credit cards in the freezer." The problem I have with much of their advice is that they tend to blame the credit card as the problem, rather than the lack of financial control and financial education of the card user. Blaming one's credit card for their financial woes is much the same as me blaming my putter for my high golf score.

Credit and debt are very important subjects in anyone's life. Today, young people while still in school are actively solicited by credit card companies, which have often caused me to ask, Why don't we teach young people about money in school? Why do we have to wait till young people are deeply in credit card debt and in debt due to school loans before we realize that there is a problem? If you ask most young people "What is the difference between *credit* and *debt*?" I doubt many could tell you the difference, and yet we let financial profiteers educate our youth.

Consumer debt has exploded in the United States and in countries around the world. In 1990, the U.S. consumer was $200 billion deep in credit card debt. In 2005, that debt will explode to $985 billion, nearly a trillion dollars of credit card debt in just the U.S. alone. That does not include the national debt—the U.S. is the largest debtor nation in the world—nor the debt many financial institutions have exposure to worldwide. How much more credit can we continue to extend to allow the consumer to accrue more debt? I do not know. If we come to the day when the U.S. consumer has more *debt* than *credit*, the world's economy will probably begin to implode. When the world begins to call its loans, when people and organizations are not able to pay their bills and credit becomes tight, many more financial problems will surface than just our individual credit card balances.

So are debt and credit bad, as so many financial experts say? Absolutely not. Debt and credit are powerful financial tools that have allowed many in the world to enjoy the highest standard of living in history. Without debt and credit, we would not have such things as great cities, massive industries, airlines flying us to all parts of the world, resorts to relax at, excellent food at exciting restaurants, new cars to drive, comfortable homes to live in, and so many choices of entertainment.

So if debt and credit are not bad, then what is? In my opinion, lack of financial education and fiscal responsibility are bad. I think it tragic that my parents' generation, the World War II generation, has left massive debt for my generation; and my generation, the Vietnam era generation, has done the same to our kids. In other words, while personal credit card abuse is irresponsible, the massive bill each generation passes on to the next generation is even more irresponsible.

How the young people born after the year 2000 will pay for multiple generations of fiscal irresponsibility, I do not know. One way to keep paying for all this debt is to keep expanding credit and encouraging people to spend more and more. The June 28, 2004, issue of *Time* magazine ran an article about schools now sending kids on field trips to shopping malls, car dealerships, supermarkets, and fast-food outlets. Why? One reason is that our cash-strapped schools cannot afford to send kids on field trips to zoos, museums, or cultural events. Yet many businesses are ready and willing to pay for these field trips to start grooming new customers while they are still in school. In other words, as long as each of us keeps consuming and keeps using our credit to acquire more debt, the economy will grow and the bills of past generations will be paid. While this may be good for business and will help keep our credit and debt economy afloat, to me it sounds risky and fiscally irresponsible.

The good news is that even though most of us cannot control our national irresponsibility, we can take control of our own finances. One of the most important lessons my rich dad taught me was the wisdom of knowing there is good debt and bad debt. Simply put, rich dad said, "Good debt makes you rich and bad debt makes you poor." Unfortunately, most of the people who were cutting up their credit cards in the financial seminar I attended only had bad debt. Even more unfortunate was that the instructor leading the class only knew of bad debt. He had no idea that good debt existed. To him, all debt was bad. Bad financial education is the cause of poor financial management.

One of the reasons this book is so important is that it is important to be financially responsible and to use the power of your credit and debt intelligently. Before turning you loose into this book, I would like to pass on three bits of information my rich dad taught me years ago. They are:

1. *Bad debt is easier to get than good debt.* If any of you have ever tried to get a loan to buy a rental property or to start a business, you may know how difficult it is to get a loan for investments. Yet if you want a car loan or a new credit card, credit, debt, and money are easy to come by, even if you have horrible credit.

2. *Bad debt makes it harder to get good debt.* If you have too much bad debt, and you want to begin using the power of debt and credit more intelligently, like for starting a business or investing in rental property, bad debt makes it harder for you to get the good debt and hence to become richer. One big reason this book is so important is that getting rid of your bad debt is an important step toward you becoming richer and more financially free.

3. *Debtors can get rich faster than savers.* Many people think that saving is better than borrowing. In fact, I know that many people work hard to save money and get out of debt. In reality, it is those who save and get out of debt who fall behind those that borrow and get into debt.

Let me use an example to explain this last statement. In 2002, my wife, Kim, purchased a commercial building for approximately $8 million. She put $1 million down and borrowed $7 million dollars. The million-dollar down payment came from accrued gains in her other investments, so technically, the $8 million purchase was a nothing down investment. This investment alone puts approximately $30,000 a month in her pocket. While many people do not make $30,000 a year, her private company makes this in a month.

To people who are savers and debt averse, I often ask them, "How long would it take you to save $7 million?" For most people, saving $7 million is out of their reality. I then ask Kim how long it took her to borrow $7 million.

Her reply is, "It took me about two weeks. Because it was such a great real estate investment, several bankers wanted to give me the money."

That is an example explaining why a debtor can get richer faster than a saver. Not only is the debtor getting richer, but the saver is getting poorer. Due to inflation and the irresponsible printing of more and more money, your dollars in savings are going down in value each year, while the debtor's property is often going up in value. A person who had $10,000 in savings in 2000 actually had only $7,000 in savings by 2003 because their U.S. dollars lost that much value. So savers lost and debtors who invested in real estate won. Of course, if the whole financial house of cards comes down, which it could, then the savers would win and the banks would get their real estate back.

The reason Garrett Sutton's book is so important is that, like it or not, debt is a powerful force in our world today. The financially intelligent are using debt to enrich themselves while the financially uneducated or irresponsible are using debt to destroy their lives. There is good debt and bad debt in this world. A very important lesson in one's life is to know how to minimize bad debt and responsibly use good debt to one's advantage. This is especially true in today's financially changing world.

Years ago, after cutting up my credit card, I realized how important my rich dad's lessons on debt and credit have been to me. That day, in the seminar, I realized that many of the participants should have cut up their credit cards. But cutting up your credit cards will not necessarily make you richer. A credit card is a very powerful tool, and that is why I love my credit card because I would rather have its power than be without its power. For a more enriched life, one must learn to respect the power of debt and credit, and learn how to use that power.

—Robert Kiyosaki

Chapter I

Credit and Debt

Donny

Donny protected his country. As a firefighter trained to fight large forest fires he was sent around the country to protect people and property from the forces of nature. Americans could go about their daily business, could sleep safe at night with their families because of Donny and his firefighting unit, experts at fighting wildfires, preserving forests, and protecting family homes. He felt satisfaction in knowing what he did mattered.

Donny was a recent college graduate. Like over a third of all college graduates he had $20,000 in student loan debt to pay off. Like over half of all college students he had more than two credit cards with an unpaid balance of over $2,000. In Donny's case the amount was $4,500. His first card had been burdened with charges to impress a worthy coed. The relationship didn't last. The debt did. His second card was from a national department store chain. He received 10 percent off everything in the store when he applied for the card. He was still paying off several of the shirts he no longer wore.

Donny had recently financed the purchase of a new Ford F-150. It was a great truck he needed to have. He was certain he could make all of the payments. The local fire department paid him like clockwork.

Donny was sent to fight a huge summer fire in Oregon. Another mission, another job to do. In the past, when on the fire lines, Donny had always been able to receive his bills and make payments on a timely basis. Then a white powder was found on an envelope at his local post office. It was anthrax. The post office was shut for three weeks while the matter was carefully investigated. The mail didn't move for another six weeks.

Donny didn't receive his bills. Meanwhile, the Oregon wildfire threatened towns and property in all directions. He was on the lines for seemingly the entire summer. Like all the other firefighters in his unit, he assumed that the creditors were aware of the situation and would arrange a grace period for payment. After all, they were serving their country.

But the creditors didn't care what Donny was doing. He was now two payments late on all his bills. That was all that mattered. Explanations, whether reasonable, justified, or good, were just excuses. And all excuses were bad.

Donny's credit card had a Universal Default Clause, one of the most odious of all credit traps. By being one day late on any payment to any creditor, the credit card company could charge a default rate on any existing balance of up to 29.99 percent. This meant that in Donny's case he had to pay an extra $2,500 a year for being one month late on another creditor's bill.

Donny missed two car payments while fighting the huge Oregon fire and the F-150 was repossessed. Because he had just purchased it, the money owed far exceeded the artificially low value it was sold for at auction.

Finally the horrendous Oregon wildfire was brought under control. Donny and scores of other firefighters returned home from a very difficult mission. In gratitude, the country's financial establishment unleashed a torrent of debt collection sharks on the returning heroes.

The firefighters were incensed. They had served their country. Through no fault of their own the mail had been delayed. Under such circumstances a little leeway was appropriate. If they were in the military, the Service Members Civil Relief Act would have shielded them from credit sharks. Why shouldn't firefighters be equally protected? But the creditors didn't care. They had rules and standards. And they made a great deal of money when people were late in paying. Some of the firefighters were now being forced into bankruptcy. Many lost their homes; many had their futures seriously delayed. A number of them wrote their congressmen demanding relief from the ingratitude of the nation's credit establishment. But individual firefighters don't contribute to Congress. Credit card companies, leasing companies, banks, and other lenders spend millions and millions of dollars to influence Congress. There was no contest.

Donny was forced to declare bankruptcy. The next seven years were financial hell. He couldn't borrow to buy a house or start a business. He had a black mark on his record he worried about and worked every day to overcome.

All for the privilege of serving his country.

Dewey

Dewey liked to play the angles. If there was an opportunity for him to take advantage of a situation or of someone else he would do so. Especially if it meant easy money without the need for work.

Recently, Dewey had turned to new credit card and bank account deals. The FBI called it identity theft, and claimed it was the fastest growing crime in America. Dewey preferred to call it selective borrowing, and it was so easy and so lucrative he wished he'd known about it sooner.

Dewey had learned that by obtaining someone's Social Security number along with basic personal information he could obtain a credit card and a bank account. The accounts would be in the unsuspecting person's name but available for the use and benefit of Dewey, who moved from city to city to ply his special talents.

Dewey had just obtained the personal information from an elderly gentleman named John Logan. It was all so easy. He called up Mr. Logan pretending to be a utility company representative. He said he needed the information to update the company's files. Mr. Logan was all too nice and willing and forthcoming.

Dewey's friend could forge a driver's license to perfection. His friend's business used to be geared for underaged teens who wanted to go bar hopping. The market now was for sharpies like Dewey. With Dewey's photo and driver's license carrying John Logan's information and an address controlled by Dewey, the plan was put in motion. Dewey opened a bank account in John Logan's name. He paid a few small bills and maintained good credit for a time. Then Dewey obtained a credit card in Logan's name. All was ready to prime the credit pump.

With the credit card Dewey bought as much electronics as the card would allow. TVs, stereos, and computers were easily fenced for cash. Dewey felt no remorse. The credit card companies and the national electronics retail chain made more than enough money. They could easily afford Dewey's hit. So could old Mr. Logan for that matter.

With his bank account Dewey wrote a large number of checks on one weekend to a number of small retail outlets around town. The smaller stores didn't have the ability to check cash availability. It was the weekend. The banks were closed. They took down John Logan's driver's license information and Dewey loaded up a rental U-Haul truck with his purchases.

By the time the checks started bouncing Dewey was hundreds of miles away getting ready for his next selective borrowing.

Unlike the credit card charges, which were absorbed by the credit card company and passed on to consumers around the world in the form of higher prices, the small retailers Dewey hit were not so lucky. When the bounced checks came back the retailer was responsible. They were out the money they paid for the goods they handed over to Dewey.

This type scam also costs the John Logans of the world dearly. The calls from the creditors and collection agencies, even when one is innocent, take their toll. The crushing financial and resulting emotional stress of a stolen identity is too much for many to take. For John Logan a stroke followed. He died shortly thereafter.

The cases of Donny and Dewey serve to illustrate the extremes and the ironies of credit and debit issues.

The credit industry actively entices all comers, especially the young and inexperienced, with the promise of credit. Critics charge their aggressive practices border on predatory lending, taking unfair advantage of those who shouldn't be borrowing. Whatever the case, the easy availability of credit encourages two types of people to sign up who shouldn't: those represented by Donny and those represented by Dewey.

Donny, fresh from college with student loans, two credit cards, and a truck payment, is starting his career on the edge of the credit abyss. If he doesn't work he is in trouble. Dewey, always ready to play the angles, has found a career taking advantage of the credit industry's willingness to lend, allowing him to work causing trouble. To combat the Deweys of the world the credit industry responds with rules and a rigidity that moves the Donnys closer to the abyss. One missed payment, anytime, for any reason, be it anthrax or cows in the road slowing the mail, and the machinery of negative credit starts to grind. A free fall ensues. Lives are ruined.

The irony of this scenario is how the credit industry treats each individual. Dewey is a cost of doing business. His fraud is known and accounted in their budgets as an expense factor. The cost is spread out over the entire industry with millions and millions of consumers footing the bill as increased costs.

Donny, on the other hand, the deserving and ethical individual and a victim of circumstance, is a casualty of doing business. He had his chance, argue industry experts, and he missed a payment. He will be punished until he can be trusted once again.

And so in this upside-down world where criminality is a cost and inadvertence amounts to a crime it is important to know the rules, the motivations, and the road map for winning with credit.

Chapter II

The Psychology of Debt

Before tackling the rules of debt and how to win with credit it is important to understand the psychology of debt. What are the motivations that lead to debt? Why are some people consistently unable to manage debt? What is the relationship between self-esteem and debt?

And why is consumer debt in America, excluding mortgages, but including credit cards, auto loans, and the like, now over $18,000 per household? With $2 trillion in aggregated debt (up from $780 billion in 1992), a record 1.5 million households filing for bankruptcy in 2003, and a declining savings rate, why are we spending like there is no tomorrow?

In my experience there are four types of borrower profiles:

Wishers
Wasters
Wanters, and
Winners

The first three profiles tend to overlap, as we'll see. The fourth profile, the winners, have either survived and moved past the difficulties of the first three categories, or were credit winners to begin with. This book will teach you how to be a credit winner.

Wishers

Wishers are credit optimists. They have the sunny perception that they deserve the good things; that they are meant to keep up with the Joneses, and can easily afford it all. In their happy dreamworld of credit optimism they focus on the monthly payments, not on the overall debt. They see a $20 payment here and a $75 payment there as doable, never focusing on the thousands of dollars of overall debt, on the crushing interest rates, they have incurred. They are convinced that they can easily pay the bills as they come due.

Such false perceptions of what can be managed are extremely problematic during the Christmas spending season, especially with the sense that the bills are due next year. Wishers, as optimists, see a brighter next year for themselves, a better job, with more income, a future whereby all money issues will be resolved.

Unfortunately, not all wishes come true.

Wasters

Wasters spend money as an escape. With low self-esteem issues, they use money to purchase things in order to feel better, relieve stress, and escape their problems. In a society where massive and pervasive advertising can easily manipulate behavior, there is nothing like the feel and sense of something new (or so the advertisers would have you believe). A new car or truck or television or vacation can end the emptiness inside—for a time. When that empty feeling returns there are still bills to pay.

Wasters, however, will continue spending. With a credit card industry that encourages, indeed programs, people to buy now (for wasters—feel now) and pay later, wasters will sign up for more credit. They will find themselves locked into a life of revolving debt. With low self-esteem they will more often declare bankruptcy and they will more often go back to their unsuccessful money management techniques of short-term retail relief and long-term debt woes.

Wanters

One of the more interesting studies in the annals of psychology is the Stanford Marshmallow Study. Begun in the 1960s, it was conducted by Walter Mischel, a Stanford University psychology researcher, and studied the importance of self-discipline on future success.

A group of hungry four-year-olds was offered a choice. They could have one marshmallow now. But if they waited fifteen or twenty minutes while the researcher ran an errand they could have two marshmallows.

A third of the children immediately ate the single marshmallow. While some waited a little longer, they ate the marshmallow before the researcher came back. The final third of the children waited the full fifteen to twenty minutes for the adult to return.

Later, when the children graduated from high school, a follow-up study provided interesting information. The impatient marshmallow eaters were less self-confident and couldn't put off immediate gratification to reach long-term goals. Their impulses were lifelong, resulting in bad marriages, low job satisfaction, and lower incomes.

The resisters, who delayed immediate gratification to receive two marshmallows, were more productive and positive in life. By being able to delay gratification in pursuit of their goals they had higher incomes, more lasting marriages, and better health.

The problem in our society is that immediate gratification is actively encouraged. Have it your way, photos or glasses or whatever in under an hour, buy now pay later are the constant messages we receive. Is it any wonder that those with lower self-discipline are lured into the indulgences of immediate gratification?

The wanters want it now and the credit industry caters to that desire. The issue of paying for all of it later inevitably becomes a problem.

Winners

Believe it or not, for all the criticism of the credit industry we have just offered, there is room for huge winnings to be realized using credit to your advantage.

The winners know this, or have learned it through their own education. Perhaps their parents imparted the knowledge or they read *Rich Dad Poor Dad, The Cashflow Quadrant*, and similar books. However the wisdom was arrived at, the formula can be rewarding. First some obvious truths:

1. Banks make money by lending money. That's their business. We all know that.

2. Banks can lose money by making loans to people or for projects that will never be paid back. Banks have to be careful. Like all of us, too many bad debts and there's trouble.

3. Banks like to make loans when they have security or collateral. If the loan isn't paid they want to latch on to something tangible and real to secure their repayment.

4. Real estate loans are safe for banks because land and buildings offer excellent security. In almost all cases, their repayment is guaranteed.

Given these obvious truths, there is one additional obvious truth that rarely gets mentioned:

5. Banks do not make the lion's share of the money on certain loans. Credit winners who understand the system and use credit to their advantage make far more money (especially on certain real estate loans) than the banks will ever hope to make.

Appreciating this rarely discussed obvious truth can make you a lot of money too. Banks make their fair share lending money. You can make a far greater amount borrowing money for the right projects. For the right reasons.

You may be thinking at this moment that real estate and secured loans from banks are totally different from credit card offerings

Not true. A few years ago my partner and I came across a quarter acre of raw land with highway frontage in Silver Springs, Nevada. The owner needed $5,000 quickly and there wasn't time to arrange for traditional bank financing. Credit cards came to the rescue. We knew we could each handle an extra $200 per month payment in order to pay off the loan in a reasonable time period. So we each took a $2,500 cash advance on our credit cards and bought the land.

In this case, the credit card company made a reasonable amount of money at their usual high interest rates and we have since paid off the principal amount. But the land has significantly appreciated and the area is ready to take off. No one can guess how much it will be worth five years from now. We used our credit cards to make a lot more money than the credit card company did.

Good Debt Makes You Rich

Good debt involves someone else paying off the debt for you. An excellent example of good debt is a real estate investment loan in which a tenant pays rental income in excess of the mortgage and related expenses. An SBA (Small Business Administration) loan that allows your business to grow is another example of good debt (so long as your business can pay it off). The best loans are nonrecourse loans, which require no personal guarantees. Good debt leads to wealth.

Bad Debt Makes You Poor

Bad debt is something you pay off yourself. Credit cards, car loans, consumer loans, and home mortgages are examples of bad debt. Some bad debt is better than other bad debt. For example, buying a personal residence is in most cases better than buying a car on credit. And while we are not saying that you shouldn't buy a personal residence on credit, you must remember that a home mortgage is a bad debt because you yourself must pay it off. Bad debt takes money from your pocket, making you poorer and poorer.

Credit winners use good debt to their advantage. And that's the purpose of this book. To get rid of negative credit habits, and start positively using credit to your advantage. But before you start winning with credit we have your health to think about . . .

Chapter III

The Health Effects of Debt

Sick of Debt

Everyone in debt knows that debt can make you feel sick. You plan around it; you think about it; you worry about it. Many of us can trace our level of stress right back to our level of debt. A study at Ohio State University found that people who reported higher levels of stress in regard to their debt showed higher levels of physical impairment and reported worse health than their counterparts with lower levels of debt. The study also found that the level of credit card debt compared to income also played a role, with those with higher percentages of debt to income reporting a higher level of physical impairment.

Debt stress impacts our relationships as well as our physical and mental health. The divorce rate is well over 50 percent and reportedly the number one reason for divorce is financial trouble. Couples argue more about money than any other relationship issue.

Stress, anxiety, and depression are common for those with uncomfortable amounts of debt. Feelings of guilt, shame, and failure all impact self-esteem and lead people to feel as if they are out of control or powerless. Add to this the fears of what will happen if the bills are not paid, the aggressiveness of many creditors and debt collectors, and the constant pressure to continue spending, and it is no wonder that some Americans actually end up taking their own lives as a means to ending the spiraling feelings.

Debt stress has also been linked to substance abuse and the accompanying health problems (including an increased risk of violence) associated with this illegal activity. On the legal side of substance abuse, many people react to stress by abusing alcohol or legal prescription drugs. Spending has become such a problem for some people that the pharmaceutical industry has taken notice. Shopping has long been recognized as an addiction for those whose spending interferes significantly with their lives. In fact, it is estimated that 8 percent of American adults (90 percent of these being women) suffer from this addiction. Research has shown that this compulsive spending is linked to low serotonin levels in the brain. Drugs that increase serotonin are now being tested to treat compulsive shopping.

Another serious health concern related to financial problems is the fact that people will often forgo treatment for physical (or mental) illness in an attempt to control debt. This too often leads to more serious ailments and even death. In addition, those in financial turmoil are more likely to go against doctor's orders and return to work sooner in order to pay the bills—medical bills included—thus increasing their chances of reinjury or relapse.

In one 2004 survey, 63 percent of Americans said that debt was making their home lives unhappy. The online survey of 5,000 consumers by Consolidated Credit Counseling Services, a nonprofit money management organization, found that:

- 43 percent reported a debt-to-income ratio of 50 percent or more.
- 58 percent of participants stated that their credit cards were at or near their maximum credit limit.
- 62 percent of participants did not have a savings account.
- 92 percent had no emergency fund for three months of living expenses.
- 37 percent had taken cash advances from one credit card to make monthly payments on another credit card.

- 59 percent paid only the minimum amount due on credit cards each month.

According to the Consolidated study, a major problem is that people assume that they are doing well because they can afford the minimum payments each month. Which of course ignores the total amount of debt and the high interest rates. When the total debt is added up, however, they are not doing well, and their stress level creeps upward.

Financial Stress Leads to Job Stress

Financial stress accounts for reduced job productivity in an estimated 15 percent of workers (as high as 50 percent at some jobs). The stress doesn't just come from worries over whether a person has enough money, either. Stress can accumulate as an individual continues to make bad financial decisions, such as spending more than one has, ignoring bills, writing bad checks, and going over credit limits. These behaviors can lead to repossessions, late notices, late fees, harassment from collection agencies, or even bankruptcy.

Anyone who has ever tried to juggle the stress of a job with the stress of financial insecurity knows that the two are bound to collide. We find ourselves being distracted on the job, missing deadlines, missing work, or actually getting sick as the stress chips away at the well-being of our minds and bodies.

Financial problems often lead workers to waste the time they are getting paid to work. They're distracted, have more trouble concentrating, and use the business phone, fax, and/or computer to deal with the financial problems—all on the boss's dime. Studies have shown that all those dimes would be better used educating the workforce about finances.

Researchers say that when the sex is good it only accounts for about 10 percent of the health of the marriage. When it's bad it accounts for about 90 percent. The same can be said for money and work. When the money is good it accounts for only about 10 percent of a person's problems. But when it's bad it accounts for 90 percent.

We all know about the connection between stress and illness. Get stressed and you get sick. Anyone who has ever gotten sick right after a big test or after the deadline for a huge project knows how stress wears us down. We get stressed; we get sick; and our employers pay—through time off from work, medical insurance claims, even higher employee turnover. If the employer does not offer insurance, the problems can escalate as injured workers try to deal with the added stress of medical bills. The original medical problem may cause the stress and the stress erodes the health and leads to further medical problems and the job suffers. Whether the stress or the medical issue precipitates the problem, the result is too often the same—reduced productivity. And just as workplace physical wellness programs have been shown to increase worker productivity, so have financial wellness programs.

Unfortunately, many people don't know where to turn when they have credit problems. This book is designed to help you understand your options so you can take control of your financial life. Let's look at how a smart and resolute couple managed to do it . . .

Chapter IV

Beat the Lenders at Their Own Game

How We Got Out of Debt—Robert and Kim Kiyosaki's Story

While Robert and Kim enjoy tremendous financial success now, they too have experienced their share of tough times. This is their story, as told by Kim:

In 1985, Robert and I had a great deal of bad debt—that is, consumer debts. And even though we kept making payments every month we never seemed to make a dent in the amount we owed. Each month we paid a little over the minimum on each of our credit cards as well as on our car loan. Obviously there had to be a better way to get ourselves out from under our creditors. And sure enough there was.

This is the formula Robert and I followed to pay off our debt. You'll find that if you follow our formula you will be out of debt much quicker than you imagined. Most people find themselves bad-debt-free within five to seven years. The key is to stick with the formula.

You will not get ahead if you say I'll just skip this month, and then two, and then three. If you stick with the formula it then becomes a habit you follow for a lifetime.

Here is the formula we used:

Step #1: Stop accumulating bad (consumer) debt. Whatever you purchase via credit cards must be paid off in full at the end of each month. No exceptions.

Step #2: Make a list of all of your consumer (bad) debts. This includes all credit cards, car loans, school loans, home improvement loans on your personal residence, and any other bad debts you have acquired. (One item on my and Robert's list was an outstanding debt to a partner from one of Robert's past businesses.) You can even include your home mortgage on this list.

Step #3: Next to each item listed make three columns:

- Amount Owed (Current Balance)
- Minimum Monthly Payment
- Number of Months to Pay Off

Enter the appropriate numbers into each column. To arrive at the number of months to pay off, simply divide the amount owed by the minimum payment. But note that credit card companies use declining minimum payments. As your balance goes down, your payment goes down, which may affect the math here.

Step #4: Based solely on the number of months, begin ranking each debt. Put a 1 next to the lowest number of months, a 2 next to the second-lowest number, and continue up to the highest number of months. This is the order that you will be paying off your various debts.

The reason you start with the debt with the lowest number of months is that you want to have your first win or success in the program as soon as possible. Once you get that first credit card (or debt) paid off you'll begin to see the light at the end of the tunnel.

Step #5: Come up with an additional $150 to $200 per month. If you are serious about getting out of debt, and more importantly, becoming financially free, then generating this extra money will not be difficult. To be candid, if you cannot generate an additional $150 per month then your chances of becoming financially independent are slim. (You may need some of the resources in the next chapter to help you get back on track.)

Step #6: Pay the minimum amount on every debt that you have listed except for the one you've marked with a 1. On this first debt to be paid off, pay the minimum amount due plus the additional $150 to $200. Keep doing this every month until your first debt is paid off. Scratch that debt from your list.

Step #7: Congratulate yourself!

Step #8: Pay the minimum amount due on every debt that you have listed except for the one you've marked with a 2. To this debt, pay the minimum amount due plus the entire amount you've been paying on debt #1. For example, on debt #1 your minimum amount due was $40, and you added the additional $150, so you were paying a total of $190 each month. On debt #2, if the minimum amount due is $50, you will now pay that $50 plus $190, for a total of $240 per month.

After each debt is paid off, take the total you were paying on that debt and add it to the minimum amount due on your next debt to get your new monthly payment. You will be amazed at how quickly this amount adds up and how quickly your credit cards, car loans, and so on are paid off.

Continue this process until all the debts on your list are paid off.

Step #9: Congratulate yourself again!

Step #10: By this time the monthly payment you were paying on your last debt is likely to be quite substantial. Keep paying that amount every month. Except now, instead of paying it to your creditors, you can pay it to yourself and build an emergency savings fund and then start investing. You're on your way to building wealth!

Start Your Own Debt-Free Plan

The method Robert and Kim describe is powerful. In fact, you may be able to slash the amount of time and money it takes to pay off your debt dramatically. For example, let's say you have the following debts:

Lender	APR	Amount Owed (Current Balance)	Minimum Monthly Payment
Visa	15.9%	$4,150	$58
MasterCard	12.9%	$3,645	$73
Retail card	18.9%	$4,595	$115
Installment loan	17.5%	$1,990	$50
Total		$14,380	$296

Guess how long it will take you to pay off that $14,380 debt if you are making the minimum payments required by the credit card company.

Only 182 years and one month!

And you'll pay over $72,000 in interest! In biblical times the lender would be stoned to death for such usury!

How can those numbers possibly be so high? In a nutshell, it's due to tiny minimum payments that go down as your balance goes down. Unlike a car loan where you'll have a fixed payment that will pay off your loan in, say, four or five years, credit card issuers figure your monthly payments as a percentage of the amount you owe. The minimum payment is already small, which is great when you need to make a small payment, but terrible when you can't pay more. As you pay down the balance, the monthly payment goes down and the debt gets s-t-r-e-t-c-h-e-d out.

The debt payoff acceleration strategy that Robert and Kim used has several powerful elements, and I've added one more tip to the mix to help make you successful even faster. Here's why it works:

1. **You keep your total monthly payment fixed.** This the first way to beat the card issuers at their own game. In our example, the total monthly payment is $296. As you pay down your debts, the amount your credit card issuer

will require you to pay will become smaller. But you won't fall for it! You'll pay at least $296 each month until all the debts are paid. Just doing that alone cuts the repayment period from 182 years and one month down to just under fifteen years and saves you over $63,000 in interest. You can put down that rock.

2. **You stop charging.** If you must have a card for business purposes only, keep it out of the plan. You've heard the saying: If you're in a hole, stop digging!

3. **You add extra if you can.** If you can afford an extra $50 a month on our example, you'll be debt-free in just five years and you'll save over $65,000 in interest. Whew!

4. **You target only one debt at a time.** If you try to do too many things at once you'll lose focus and won't get anywhere. If you focus on paying one debt off at a time, you'll be much more successful. For maximum savings, you should target the highest-rate debt first. However, if you're like Kim and Robert and want to see some fast results, focus on the lowest balance first.

5. **You'll have a plan.** Research by the Consumer Federation of America and the Bank of America found that people with as little as $10,000 a year in income who reported having a written plan had twice as much money in savings and investments as those without a plan. The same principle applies when you are getting out of debt. Having a written plan can give you that discipline and motivation you need.

Here are several different strategies for reducing debt as illustrated by the Debt Reduction Report below:

Debt Reduction Report

Complete Debt Summary

Number of Debts	4
Start Month	April 2004
Payment Plan	Immediate
Payoff Strategy	APR
Balance Owed	$14,380
Monthly Payments	$296
Pledge Money	$50
Payments + Pledge	$346

Minimum Payment from Statement	
Debt-Free Date	April 2186
Months Required	2185
Total Interest Paid	$72,333
Total Money Paid	$86,713

Minimum Payment Held Constant	
Debt-Free Date	December 2022
Months Required	225
Total Interest Paid	$14,209
Total Money Paid	$28,589
Money Saved	**$58,124**
Time Saved	**163 years 4 months**

Debt Blaster without Pledge Money	
Debt-Free Date	November 2010
Months Required	80
Total Interest Paid	$9,169
Total Money Paid	$23,549
Money Saved	**$63,164**
Time Saved	**175 years 5 months**

Debt Blaster with Pledge Money	
Debt-Free Date	April 2009
Months Required	61
Total Interest Paid	$6,645
Total Money Paid	$21,025
Money Saved	**$65,688**
Time Saved	**177 years 0 months**

Debt Blaster™ Copyright 1991–1997 by Michael J. Riley, Preprinted with permission. Available through SuccessDNA.com.

Here's a brief explanation of the various repayment strategies described in the Debt Reduction Report:

- **Minimum Payment from Statement:** This example shows how much you would pay, and how long it would take to get out of debt, if you made only the issuer's required minimum payments each month. As explained above, your minimum required payments decline as your balance goes down, stretching out the debt for a long time.

- **Minimum Payment Held Constant:** Here's how long it would take to pay off your debt if you continued making the minimum payments currently required by your statement. This corresponds with Robert and Kim's instructions about dividing the balance by the current minimum payment. It's faster than paying the declining minimum payments and will save you money in the long run.

- **Debt Blaster without Pledge Money:** This describes how long it would take you to pay off the debt if you turbocharge your payment plan as we described. You stick with the same total monthly payment that you must make now, but as you pay down some debts you put the "extra" amount above the minimum payment toward the highest rate debt until it's paid off, and so on.

• **Debt Blaster with Pledge Money:** If you can add some extra money toward your total monthly payment you'll get out of debt faster. In this example, we added just $50 per month but saved much more than that in interest.

What you're doing here is creating a tsunami effect. It will seem very slow at first, but as soon as you start paying off a debt or two your plan will pick up speed and you'll start seeing dramatic effects.

If you've ever had a mortgage you probably noticed that in the first several years most of your payment went toward interest, not principal (principal is the amount you borrowed). But several years into the loan it starts shifting and near the end your payment is mostly principal, not interest. Why does most of the interest get paid off first? Because so many people refinance long before the loan is paid off. Nowadays lenders want to earn as much interest as possible in the loan's early years. They don't make money when you pay off principal, so the principal payments are very low at the start and only grow once most of the interest (read, profit) has been paid off.

Turbocharge Your Debt-Free Plan

The lower your interest rate, the faster you'll get out of debt. Many people are trapped in high-rate credit card debt these days, at interest rates ranging from 19.98 percent to 29.99 percent or even higher. In fact, if you have run up large balances you are more likely to see your interest rates skyrocket.

Why? Because most issuers realize that when you have a lot of debt you won't be able to get another low-rate card. So they raise your interest rate, knowing you're stuck. In addition, about one third of credit card issuers now include the Universal Default Clause in their credit card agreements, which allows them to raise your interest rate on existing balances and future purchases if you are just one day late with a payment to them—or if you are late with *any* bill that appears on your credit report! The more debt you have, the more likely you are to be paying high interest rates. (Unlike other businesses, in the world of consumer credit, you don't get a discount for volume.)

You'll turbocharge your plan if you try to get the lowest rates possible. As you start to pay off your credit cards, you should constantly be looking for ways to lower your interest rates.

Scott Bilker is the author of *Talk Your Way Out of Credit Card Debt* (www.debtsmart.org). He has made and recorded hundreds of calls with banks in his efforts to lower interest rates for himself, family, and friends. In his book, he uses this real-life illustration:

He made 52 phone calls that took 403 minutes (6 hours, 43 minutes) and saved $43,147.68. That's an average savings of $107.07 per minute. Wouldn't you like to save over a hundred bucks a minute? Even $100 per hour is good.

So how do you lower your interest rate? Well, you can ask. You get on the phone and start asking your card issuers to lower your rates. They may or may not, but you won't know unless you try. As my father (and yours too, probably) always said: "It never hurts to ask." So, go ahead, stand tall and ask for a rate reduction.

The main reason card issuers will often negotiate with you is because they want to keep cardholders with balances. After all, that's how they make money. Many times they'd rather lower your interest rate than lose you as a customer. Of course this means you're not going to call and threaten to pay off your entire balance unless they lower your rate. What incentive does the issuer have there? None. So state that you're better able to make the monthly payments with a lower rate. That's what they want to hear. Then, when you get the lower rate, work to pay off the entire balance.

Many people are intimidated by the thought of negotiating with their credit card company. There is no need to feel this way. Just remember the other thing my father always said: "He who cares least, wins."

You can be sure that the credit card company really doesn't care about you as an individual, or about your unique concerns and issues. You are a billing unit, one of millions of indistinguishable billing units. You exist merely to provide profit. And let's be honest, if you ran the company you'd see it that way too.

So if they care that little about you (and they do care—that little), why then should you care what they think about you?

Be assured that the customer service representative you speak with won't remember you an hour later. They speak with hundreds and hundreds of people every day. Do you really think that they go home at night and gossip about the embarrassing credit problems John in Des Moines is experiencing? Don't flatter yourself. The fact is, your customer service representative these days probably lives in India and goes home at night worrying about sanitary drinking water. How do you rate on that continuum? Drinking water . . . John in Des Moines. Your insignificant problems don't even register in their consciousness.

Now that we have the context established, stop caring what these understandably uncaring people think about you and start negotiating to your advantage. Ask for lower rates and do it without a care. They're not going to bite you or write you down for asking. They don't care. And neither do you. And by caring least about it, not worrying about it, not having one cautious doubt about it, you will win.

Another way to win is to simply transfer balances to cheaper—those with lower interest rates—cards. If you still have plenty of credit available, this can be a terrific money saver. Call each of your issuers and tell them you have credit card balances, and are shopping for the lowest rate to consolidate those balances. Ask them what they can do for you. (It's helpful to keep notes on what each one offers.) If you're not up to your eyeballs in debt, or have poor credit, you should get some very good offers. You can also shop for a new card at www.cardratings.com.

Look out for the following when you're doing this:

• Balance transfer fees can add up. Some issuers will charge a transfer fee of as much as 2 percent to 4 percent of the transfer amount. Ask about this fee and try to get it waived if it's high.

• Tiered rates. If you already have a $2,000 balance on a card at, say, 18 percent, and you transfer a new balance of, say, $1,000 at 4.9 percent, the issuer will apply your payments to paying down the 4.9 percent part of the balance first. This is the exact opposite of what I recommend if you're trying to get out of debt. There's not a lot you can do about it except try to pay off a card before transferring a new balance to it.

Ask and Receive

Jorge had been out of work for a few months and had turned to his credit cards to tide him over. When he started working again, he found himself with four credit cards and balances totaling nearly $9,000. His interest rates ranged from 12 percent to 21 percent.

He paid as much as he could each month, but with the high interest rates the balances didn't seem to budge. In addition, he had gone $400 over the limit on one card. The card company didn't turn down the purchase at the time—after all it meant they could collect a $29 overlimit fee each month while he struggled to get it under the limit.

It never occurred to Jorge to negotiate his interest rates until a friend bragged how he had gotten his credit card company down to 4.9 percent. That motivated Jorge to start dialing.

His first goal was to get the overlimit fee erased from future bills. The first person he talked to acted as though he had committed a crime by going over his limit. But Jorge stayed cool and asked to speak to a supervisor. The supervisor turned him down too.

Jorge called the next day and managed to get someone a little more sympathetic. This time he got his credit limit raised so the fee automatically went away. And the interest rate dropped from 21 percent to 12.9 percent.

He went to work on the next card, and managed to reduce the interest rate from 18 percent to 9.9 percent for six months. Although it meant he'd have to negotiate again soon, it was better than nothing.

The third card issuer offered him a low transfer rate of 6.9 percent for any balances he transferred to the card, so he used that to pay off the balance on the fourth card.

With his interest rates lowered and full-time income coming in again, Jorge created a rapid repayment plan that had his $9,000 in credit card debt paid off in just two years.

Chapter V

Debt Consolidation

Should I Get a Consolidation Loan?

The ideal scenario for someone with debt is to get a low-rate consolidation loan and pay it off in three or four years. But that's easier said than done. True consolidation loans are usually unsecured personal loans (we'll talk about other types of consolidation loans in a moment). The problem is that lenders know that if you already have quite a bit of debt and then consolidate, you're likely to end up deeper in debt in a year or two. Remember our four types of borrowers:

Wishers
Wasters
Wanters, and
Winners

Wishers, wasters, and wanters are all at risk when it comes to consolidation loans. They will often:

• Get a consolidation loan based solely on the monthly payment. Once they've consolidated, they figure they'll be able to quickly pay it off but have no specific plan for doing so.

- Soon run up new debt. After all they still need a new car, television set, clothing, and so forth.
- Be at risk for high-rate consolidation loans because they are focused just on today's situation and not on a big-picture plan for getting out of debt.

For winners, though, a consolidation loan is just a way to lower costs in order to get out of debt faster. They'll take a consolidation loan if it makes sense, but they won't fall for gimmicks like high-rate loans.

Lenders know that there are a lot of wishers, wanters, and wasters out there. That's how they make money! They also know that puts their loans at risk, especially since they don't have any collateral to go after if you don't pay.

That makes a consolidation loan hard to get if you already have quite a bit of credit card debt. You can shop for a consolidation loan, but what you're more likely to find are offers to tap the equity in your home (where lenders at least can foreclose if they really have to) or offers for credit counseling and debt settlement (which we'll talk about in the next chapter).

Home Loans for Debt Consolidation

Randy was worried about how to make ends meet. He told himself it was a temporary situation. He would be back up to credit normalcy in no time. But in the last year he had gone a bit overboard in buying a boat, a trailer, and a few fairly expensive boat trip vacations. Now he was having trouble with several high-interest credit card payments.

His friend Scott had gone through a similar stretch and had emerged unscathed. Randy asked him how he did it and learned about the 125 percent mortgage. Scott said it was great. It allowed you to borrow against your house for more than it was worth—25 percent more—and the interest payments were tax-deductible.

Randy asked Scott to help him understand by using his house as an example. Scott agreed and asked him how much the first mortgage was. Randy replied that his house was worth $100,000 and his mortgage was down to $85,000. Scott explained that 125 percent of the value of his home was $125,000, which was 25 percent above the $100,000 house price. With a first mortgage claiming the first $85,000 in equity, there was room to borrow another $40,000, which was arrived at by subtracting the $85,000 first mortgage from the $125,000 value of the home.

Randy was interested, especially when Scott mentioned that home equity loans offered much better interest rates than those of credit cards. Randy owed $30,000 at 17 percent and it was killing him. Scott gave him the name of a banker to contact.

Randy called the next day. The banker quoted an initial interest rate of 7.5 percent, which was quite favorable. While the application, title insurance, appraisal, recording and attorney's fees, points, and other closing costs were going to be $5,000, Randy could see how the consolidation of his credit card debt with a home equity loan could be of benefit. The banker took down some personal information to do a credit check. He learned that Randy worked for a large trucking company in town that was rumored to be in trouble. When the banker asked how the company was doing, Randy gritted his teeth and said fine. The banker said he needed a day to process the information. He took down some more personal information from Randy to do a credit check.

When the banker called back, he informed Randy that the interest rate would have to be 9 percent instead of 7.5 percent. Randy had missed a few payments recently, which jumped the rate. Still, the banker explained, by transferring his $30,000 credit card balances at 17 percent to a new 9 percent home equity loan, Randy could save $63,816 in interest over a five-year payoff period.

That was all Randy needed to hear. He signed the paperwork the next day. He now had an $85,000 first mortgage and a home equity loan of $35,000, which equaled the $5,000 in costs for the loan plus the $30,000 loan amount. His home, valued at $100,000, now had $120,000 in loans against it.

A month later Randy received the news he feared was coming. The trucking company was going out of business. Everyone was laid off immediately.

Randy was a logistics and distribution expert. He had graduated from the University of Nevada, Reno, the top logistics school in the country, and had marketable skills. He immediately started looking for a new job. A number of interviews soon followed, which was good for Randy, except for one thing. All of the opportunities were over 300 miles away. He would have to sell his house. The house that was worth $100,000 yet had $120,000 in loans against it.

Randy took a job 1,000 miles away that started immediately. He found a real estate broker to list his house, saying he needed a quick sale. He needed to line up an apartment in his new town and couldn't afford both a house payment and an apartment payment. The broker explained that a quick sale could net him $90,000 after closing costs and brokerage fees. Randy then explained that he had $120,000 in debt against the house. The broker informed him that a sale wouldn't close until the home equity loan was paid off. He would have to find another loan for $30,000, the difference between the $120,000 borrowed against the house and the $90,000 he would net on its sale.

Randy was stuck, almost. Fortunately, sort of, he hadn't canceled the credit card accounts. He could put the $30,000 back on 17 percent credit cards. He cringed at the thought of paying $5,000 in points and fees for a home equity loan he used for one month. But then he remembered that his friend Scott said there were huge tax write-offs and benefits to all of this. He called Amy, a CPA he used to date in college who, incredibly, was still a friend, to get the tax answers. Amy immediately set Randy straight on the deductibility of home equity loans. A number of her clients thought there were huge tax deductions to be had. The truth was otherwise.

First, Amy explained, you can't deduct interest on the portion of a home equity loan that exceeds the home's fair market value. You can deduct the interest up to 100 percent of its value, but anything over that amount would be too good to be true, and, Amy said laughing, the IRS generally disallows anything that's too good to be fair. So the interest on the extra 20 percent in loans Randy had over the house's fair market value (or 100 percent) was not deductible.

Second, Amy noted, the mortgage interest deduction kicks in only if you itemize expenses. You don't save anything in taxes until you itemize (in 2004) more than $9,700 in itemized deductions for couples or, in Randy's case, $4,850 for singles. Even if Randy had itemized $10,000 in 2004 and he was in the 25 percent marginal bracket, his benefit wasn't $2,500. It was only 25 percent of $5,150, the difference between his deductions of $10,000 in deductions and the $4,850 deduction threshold. The huge savings would be just $1,287.50.

Third, said Amy, as only a friend could, you only had the loan for one month. How much in tax savings did you really expect?

Chagrined, Randy asked Amy for advice on his debt issues. She told him to stop taking on debt and pay off the $30,000 as quickly as possible. With a new job in a new city, she suggested he take a new approach to his finances. Amy observed that there weren't many lakes where he was headed. She noted that the only benefit he was getting from the boat right now was from the anchor. Unfortunately, it was wrapped around his neck and wallet. She suggested that Randy consider selling the boat and trailer and cutting his debt in half.

Randy realized this was a good idea.

One of the most popular ways to consolidate your debt is to use the equity in your home. If your home is worth more than you owe—and with real estate appreciating throughout the country, for many people these days it is—then you may be able to get a loan against it.

There are two basic ways to do this:

- Get a home equity loan or line of credit.
- Refinance your current loan and get "cash-out" to pay off debt.

There's always a risk—and it's a real one—that you could lose your home if you can't pay a home equity loan or the new mortgage. Recently we've seen foreclosures at an all-time high. With credit card debt, the worst that will happen if you run into tough times is that the account will be charged off and sent to collection. Eventually you may be sued. But, unlike the home equity or mortgage loans, you can't immediately lose your home just because you don't pay your credit card bill.

Home equity loans can be deceptive, since it makes it appear that you are turning bad debt into good debt. But when you trade credit card debt for home equity debt, you're giving up the opportunity to take that home equity and turn it into good debt—perhaps by leveraging it to buy investment property. Instead you're just sucking out your equity to pay for expenses and high interest rates you may have incurred long ago. Unfortunately, many people consolidate using their home and then they end up with new credit card debts a year or two later—only now their home is maxed out. Unless things are truly on the upswing for you financially, you may want to avoid putting your home at risk using this method.

Home Equity Loans

These loans come in two flavors: home equity loans that are for a fixed amount with a fixed repayment period; and home equity lines of credit, which are more like a credit card, allowing you to borrow up to a certain amount and pay it back with more flexibility.

Many home equity plans set a fixed period during which you can borrow money. At the end of this "draw" period (which might be ten years, for example), you will not be able to borrow any more money. You may have to pay the balance due then, or you may have another period (ten years, for example) during which you must repay the loan. Some plans may require you to take out a minimum amount when you first get the loan or may impose a prepayment penalty if you pay off the loan in the first or second year.

The good thing about home equity loans is that they usually carry low interest rates, the interest you do pay is usually tax-deductible if you itemize, and the payments are relatively low. Many home equity lines, for example, allow you to pay only interest each month.

They are also relatively easy to get if you have okay credit. And, best of all, they usually carry low—or even no—closing costs. You may have to pay for an appraisal, but often you don't have to pay for more than that.

If you have a good first mortgage already in place, you may want to go for a home equity loan. And when you refinance your home, you may want to obtain a home equity line of credit whether you currently need it or not, just so you have it in place. Getting one of these loans can be difficult if you are having financial problems or lose your job.

Refinancing

Another way to tap the equity in your home is to refinance. This is especially attractive if your current mortgage has a high interest rate or if you want to start over again with a new, longer mortgage.

A "cash-out" refinance allows you to refinance your mortgage, pay off the current loan, and take additional cash out to pay off debts You may be able to borrow up to 90 percent of the value of your home in a cash-out refinance, but that depends on your credit score and whether you are self-employed.

(Lower credit scores and self-employment may mean you can't borrow quite as much on a cash-out transaction.)

Why would you want to get a longer mortgage? In a simple word: leverage. Many of the new mortgages offer features like interest-only payments for the first several years, or fixed payments and rates for two to five years, followed by adjustable rates. The beauty of these loans is that you can get your payment way down, allowing you to free up monthly cash flow for other purposes.

If those other purposes are wealth-producing, such as real estate investments, then this can be a good option for you. If you plan to free up money just so you can spend more on stuff that will be gone by the time the next bill comes, why bother? You will have wasted an excellent opportunity to advance your financial future on another round of useless doodads.

Refinancing usually isn't free. Closing costs usually add up to about 4 percent of the mortgage amount. Some lenders offer no-cost refinancing, but you'll pay a higher interest rate. Again, that may not be a bad idea if you're trying to leverage your money for a wealth-producing investment.

Note: You cannot buy a home and simultaneously get a loan to both buy the home and consolidate unsecured debt. Lenders may finance up to 107 percent of the purchase price of a home, but that is to cover closing costs. Avoid loans that will lend more than that, since they're usually predatory loans. If you buy a home at below-market value, however, you may be able to get a home equity loan and use that to pay off unsecured debt, or you may be able to sell the house and use the proceeds to pay off unsecured debt.

Retirement Loans for Debt Consolidation

Edgar had several credit cards totaling about $35,000 in balances. One issuer in particular had raised his rate to 29.99 percent and wouldn't budge. That really bugged him, so Edgar decided he'd cash in his IRA and use the funds to pay off that debt. However, that was an expensive choice. First, since he had taken a tax deduction when he'd contributed to his IRA, the early withdrawal rate was subject to taxes as if it were current income, plus he had to pay a 10 percent penalty for early withdrawal. That made Edgar's strategy a costly one.

You may be able to borrow against your 401(k), 403(b), or pension account, but not against your IRA.

Most plans allow you to borrow up to 50 percent of the value of your account and pay it back over five years. Interest is charged, but it's usually at a fairly low rate and you pay it to yourself, not to a lender. Another benefit is that you don't have to have good credit to borrow, since there is no credit check. Of course there are drawbacks. The big risk if you take one of these loans through your employer-sponsored plan and then leave (or lose) your job is that you may have to pay back the loan immediately or pay the taxes and penalties as if it were an early withdrawal. Ouch!

Here's another big risk: the risk that it won't solve your problem and you'll end up in bankruptcy anyway. Let's say you've gotten yourself into a lot of debt because of pay cuts at work or a business that went under. So you start raiding your retirement funds. It takes you longer to get back on your feet than you expected. You end up in bankruptcy anyway. Now your retirement funds, which would have been protected in bankruptcy, are gone. You're literally starting from scratch.

☞ *Credit Maximizer Tip:* If your retirement money is in an IRA, talk with a tax or financial professional to find out if you are eligible to roll it over into a single 401(k) for business owners. These plans typically allow you to borrow up to 50 percent of the value of the account. They are available to owner-owned businesses with no full-time employees.

Friends and Family

Friends or family may be willing to help you out if you're in a rough spot. But please think twice before asking them to do that. Are you really sure that you can pay back the loan? Really, really sure? If not, you're just dragging them into your financial problems.

Your parents, richer older brother, or any other friend or relative do not "owe" you anything, even if they make gobs more than you do. Allowing them to bail you out may temporarily help the situation but unless your problems are truly out of the ordinary for you, the relief won't last. That's because you need to learn how to stop taking on bad debt and build wealth instead.

If you—or they—are determined to make one of these loans, then at least make it professional. Get an official promissory note and set up an official repayment schedule. And treat it as any other loan, not as a gift! Visit the Resources section for more information about how to do this properly.

Prepaying Your Mortgage

For some people a mortgage is considered good debt. That's because you're largely using the bank's money to purchase an asset that likely will increase over time. It's called leverage.

While paying off your credit cards and other bad debt should be your first priority, there are times when it can make sense to pay off your mortgage faster than the thirty-year or fifteen-year loan you've taken out.

ADVANTAGES OF PREPAYING

• You'll keep more money in your pocket. A typical home loan costs two to three times the original loan amount in interest. That's money that will be yours, instead of your banker's, if you prepay.

• You'll own your home free and clear sooner. For many people, that gives them a tremendous amount of comfort.

• Building up equity may give you more flexibility if you need to move, or even borrow against your home for other investments or a business. A highly leveraged house can quickly become a burden if times get tough.

DISADVANTAGES OF PREPAYING

• When interest rates are low on home loans, you don't get a huge bang for your buck by prepaying. (Although you may still "earn" a return greater than the paltry amount paid on savings accounts.)

• You may lose some of the tax advantages of deductible mortgage interest. Keep in mind, though, that if your interest costs and other itemized expenses don't exceed the standard deduction, you're not getting a huge deduction anyway.

• Home equity is not very liquid. It's easy to borrow against when your financial situation is fine, but run into problems and you may have trouble qualifying for a loan. (That's why it's good to line up a home equity loan *before* you really need it.)

Here's the bottom line: Pay off your bad debt first. Then make sure you have an adequate emergency savings fund, plus good insurance (health, life, disability, auto, and an umbrella policy). Then if you have extra money you'd like to use to prepay your mortgage, go ahead. Don't forget to keep focusing on wealth building rather than just debt reduction as your end goal. If prepaying your mortgage fits into that plan by all means do it!

The Key to Getting Out of Debt

Have you noticed one thing about the options we've described in this chapter? They may all help you to lower your cost and/or your payments as you get out of debt, but you still must find the money to pay them off!

There are several ways to do this:

• **Cut expenses.** Start tracking where you spend your money and look for ways to cut back. It may not be fun, but think of it as temporary. One of the best ways to do this is to start paying attention to what you're spending and see if you can find ways to cut even a little. Every extra dollar you free up can help you cut your debt faster. I've included a budget worksheet in Appendix D to help you learn where your money is going.

• **Bring in more income.** One of the best ways to do this may be to have your own business. This may save you money in taxes and bring in extra cash, as well as other benefits. Check out other books in the Rich Dad series for information on starting a new business.

Chapter VI

Getting Help

Sometimes you need more than just a payment schedule to get out of debt. If you're constantly juggling payments, robbing Peter to pay Paul, or using the credit cards to fill in the gaps in your budget, more help may be in order. Here are your options when your debt is getting to be too much.

In Deeper

Maria couldn't sleep at night. Her debts were mounting and she was having trouble paying them off. Creditors were calling late at night after she had drifted off. They were demanding payment and reawakening her daily life fears.

Maria's friend Alonzo knew of her troubles. He suggested she consider receiving the help of a credit counseling program. Alonzo didn't like to admit it but he had also gone through a tough stretch five years ago. His every waking moment was filled with worry over the future.

He was suffering from stress and unable to make basic life decisions. Fortunately, he saw an ad for a company that helped people consolidate their debt and he had called them in need.

Alonzo told Maria that the company went right to work getting the interest on his bills lowered. They came up with a reasonable payment plan.

Alonzo paid the company and the company paid the creditors. He was out of financial trouble in three years. Today he was on his way toward saving enough for a deposit to buy a house. Alonzo gave Maria the telephone number of the company and suggested that she call.

Maria called the next day, only to find that the company had gone out of business. As she was wondering what to do next she saw a television ad for a company that promised to consolidate your debts. Not wanting to bother Alonzo by telling him that his suggested solution was out of business she called the toll-free number on the TV ad.

The company's representative was very pleasant to deal with. She explained the program is like having a banker on your side to negotiate down all the excessive interest and fees that ordinary Americans end up paying to the large finance companies. The company worked with thousands of creditors, credit card companies, and national accounts and they were able to lower people's payments significantly. She also explained that Maria would not have to worry about making the payments to her creditors anymore. For a small fee, their credit counseling company would make all the necessary payments on a monthly basis. She said Maria would have the peace of mind of not having to deal directly with her creditors and that she would be able to sleep again at night.

The program sounded like a salvation for Maria. She had been worried about having to declare bankruptcy and was not at all in favor of that course of action. Her mother and father were proud people. If they learned that she had gone into bankruptcy they would disown her.

Maria decided without hesitation to sign up with the credit counseling program. She sent them the first month's fee of $500 and looked forward to a good night's sleep.

Later that evening a credit card representative called. Maria was pleased to be able to tell him that she had signed up with a credit counseling program and that they would be dealing with them from now on.

Within another half an hour the representative of a large department store chain called demanding their payment. Again, Maria told them that they would be hearing from her credit counseling program. The representative hung up in a huff. Maria felt good about her new power and enjoyed a restful sleep.

In another ten days and within minutes of each other the two creditor representatives called back. Neither the credit card company nor the department store chain had heard from the credit counseling company. Each again demanded payment. Maria was worried and responded by saying something must be wrong and that she would check right into it.

She immediately called the credit counseling program. The representative she had dealt with was no longer employed by the company. She was assigned a new equally pleasant representative. Maria was distraught and tearfully explained that creditors were still calling to demand payment. They claimed they had not heard from the company. The pleasant representative calmed Maria down and said there was nothing to worry about. She said it took fourteen to twenty days for their process to start working. She assured Maria that the creditors would soon be informed of their professional involvement and that all would be fine. Maria was assuaged but did not sleep well that night.

In another two weeks both creditors called again to demand payment. Late fees and interest payments were being assessed. Maria nervously asked if the credit counseling program had called them. Neither had heard from the company. Maria asked if they would call the company directly to confirm her involvement in their program. Neither was willing to lift a finger to dial eleven digits and call. They both said that wasn't their job. It was her job, they said, to pay her bills. She was over a month late.

Maria called the credit counseling program again. The pleasant representative assured her all was well, and then asked if Maria had sent in the next month's payment of $500. Maria replied that with all the creditors calling she had neglected to do so. The pleasant representative became a bit firm stating that the only way for the program to work was for the payments to be made on a timely basis. Maria promised to send it right in, and did so as soon as she got off the phone.

The two creditors called again in a matter of days. They both had finally heard from the credit counseling program. They both told her that she had missed last month's payments and late fees and interest were now accruing.

Maria demanded that the credit card representative explain why the charges were accumulating. The credit counseling program had taken over, he had just acknowledged as much. They were making the payments for her. There was nothing more to discuss.

The creditor said there was plenty more to discuss. He asked if she realized that the credit counseling program took their fees up front. She said she did not. He said that the reason she was a month late on her bills was that the program kept the first $500 themselves. No bills were paid by them last month.

Maria was shocked. No one had told her about this. The customer service rep laughed, saying she wasn't alone. Plenty of people had been lured in by the program only to learn later of the up-front fees feature and find themselves another month behind and even deeper in debt.

Maria started crying. The creditor caller softened his nasty tone and asked if she could make the smallest of minimum payments on the credit card. Maria between tears said she couldn't. She had just sent the second payment to the credit counseling program. It was all she could afford without losing her apartment.

The creditor caller asked her to call the credit counseling program again. Typically they only handled debts in place the second month into the program, once their up-front fees were paid. He suggested that maybe she could persuade them to make the minimum payment on the overdue credit card.

Maria thanked him for his suggestion. She immediately called the credit counseling program. Again she was reassured that everything was just fine.

But Maria was being told she was now two months behind on her payments. She was suffering from too much stress to make a rational decision. Without telling her friends or family she declared bankruptcy. All for $15,000 in debts.

Credit Counseling

You've no doubt seen the ads for companies promising to "consolidate your debt." Often these ads are for credit counseling agencies. These agencies have been around for many years, as something of a last resort for consumers in debt.

Here's what happens when you enter one of these programs:

They will collect information about your debts and finances. They then fill out a proposal for each of the creditors and get them to agree to reduced interest and/or fees—in most cases, but not all. You'll have a payment plan proposal to get you out of debt in three to six years in most cases.

When you enter a counseling program, you'll typically make one monthly payment to the agency, which then pays all your participating creditors. It's not true consolidation in the sense that you're still on the hook for all the original debts. If the agency doesn't make your payments, guess who's still responsible?

In addition, some types of debts can't be included, such as student loans, tax debts, mortgages, car loans, and some others. The agency may have other programs to help you with those debts but they typically can't be included in a counseling program.

There are hundreds of counseling agencies across the country. Some lenders work with over seven hundred agencies! What that means for you is that you shouldn't expect that each of your individual payment plans will be "negotiated" with your lender. Instead, the lender will have policies about what it offers for consumers in counseling. Some major card issuers, for example, will drop the interest rate to zero for consumers in counseling, while others won't drop it at all. It depends on each creditor.

Typically, you end up paying anywhere from 1.2 to 1.5 times your original debt by the time you complete the program. So if you start the program owing $10,000, you'll probably pay between $12,000 and $15,000 by the time the program is done. That may be a _bargain_ compared to the amount you would have paid if you hadn't gone this route and just continued to make minimum payments. Again, it depends on what interest rates you'll pay on each of your debts and how long it takes you to complete your program.

When credit counseling doesn't work for consumers, it's for a variety of reasons.

Sometimes consumers just aren't realistic about their debt situation. They sign up for a counseling program agreeing to a monthly payment that gives them very little breathing room in their budget. Then they have a couple of emergencies and they can't keep up with the program. Remember, it usually takes three to six years to complete a counseling program. While you're in the program you won't have access to new credit, which is what you probably relied on in the past for emergencies.

Another big problem is consumers may get sucked in by a counseling agency that charges high fees or doesn't make the payments to creditors on time. When either happens you may find yourself deeper in debt.

How Does Counseling Affect Your Credit Report?

This is likely the number one question many consumers ask about going into credit counseling. If you've been paying your bills on time, you may be worried that your good credit will quickly become bad credit. Here are some things you should understand:

Even if you pay every bill on time, your credit may not be as stellar as you think. A 2004 study by Experian Consumer Direct found that:

- More than 16 percent of the U.S. population use at least 50 percent of their available credit.
- The national average credit score for those with credit card utilization of at least 50 percent is 631 compared to the overall national average of 678.

You'll learn more about how credit scores work in the second half of this book, but suffice to say that if you're maxed out, your credit score may be hurting as a result. Reducing your debt can help improve your credit.

The popular FICO scores don't count against you for being in credit counseling when calculating your score (again, you'll learn more about FICO scores later in this book).

Most creditors will "re-age" your account once you've made three successful on-time payments through the counseling agency. That means they will delete late payments immediately before you enter the program.

Counseling agencies have come under fire in recent years for charging excessive fees, abusing their nonprofit status by funneling money to for-profit affiliates, and for misleading consumers about their programs. In fact, in 2003 the Federal Trade Commission sued one of the largest counseling agencies for just those reasons, and in 2004 the U.S. Senate held hearings on abusive counseling agencies. They found that some of the agencies were abusing both their tax-exempt status as well as consumer trust.

That doesn't mean all counseling agencies are bad. In fact, some have quietly been doing a lot of good work for many years on relatively small budgets. A good counseling agency may be able to help you avoid bankruptcy and further problems. [For direction to a reputable agency, visit www.successdna.com.] But, just as in Maria's case, you will want to choose one *very* carefully.

Debt Settlement

Although it's not really brand-new, this method for getting out of debt is not well known to many people. It's becoming increasingly popular, however, for financially strapped consumers who can't get out of debt on their own, but can't—or don't want to—file bankruptcy to arrange for the services of a debt settlement company.

Here's what it involves:

You stop making your payments to your unsecured creditors. Instead you start making a regular monthly payment to a separate savings account. (These payments are typically lower than the minimum payments you probably have been making.) After your debts go unpaid for several months, they will typically be charged off by your lenders. That means the lenders write them off their books as bad debts, but they can still try to collect on them.

At the same time, you will build up your savings account. At that point, the company will negotiate settlements on your debts—sometimes as low as 25 cents on the dollar, but usually in the 50 percent to 75 percent range.

Under most programs, you will be completely out of debt (at least unsecured debt) in anywhere from twelve to thirty-six months depending on your total debt. Twenty-four months is a typical program. Your total payoff will usually be 50 percent to 60 percent of the amount of debt that you entered the program with, including the fees charged by the settlement company.

So if you have $20,000 in debt, you might enter a debt settlement program calling for two years of $500 monthly payments. After twenty-four months at $500 a month you would have paid $12,000 including fees to settle your debts, or just 60 percent of the $20,000 originally due. Of course the final numbers will depend on your individual situation but the plan can work in certain cases.

A few things to keep in mind about debt settlement:

• You need to make sure the money you send in for your savings account to settle your debt is held in a separate trust account away from the debt settlement companies' operating funds.

• You'll want the company to handle calls from creditors. In most cases, they will get a limited power of attorney to be able to communicate with your creditors for you. This can alleviate the harassment you may be experiencing if you are falling behind.

• You may be liable for taxes on any debt forgiven by your creditors. Many consumers in a hardship situation are able to get those taxes waived by the IRS, but you'll want to get advice from a tax professional.

• Debt settlement is for consumers in a hardship situation, not for those who just don't want to pay back their debts or pay high interest rates. The debt settlement company should qualify you based on your financial picture.

One of the most common fears people face when considering debt settlement is the fear that they are somehow immorally wiggling out of debts they legitimately owe. Don't be so harsh on yourself.

First of all, there is nothing immoral about paying back as much as you can. Life happens and people run into problems. The credit card companies know, when they extend huge credit lines and hike up interest rates to 25 percent plus, that some people won't be able to pay them back. They are still enormously profitable.

Secondly, if you are in a hardship situation and don't take this step, then your next option will likely be bankruptcy. In that case, your creditors may get nothing.

So do what you have to do. Pay what you can. Then get on with your life so you can focus on building wealth, which benefits our entire economy (including the credit card companies!).

Settling

Rick's dream was to open a restaurant, and at the age of twenty-seven, he turned it into a reality. His good sense of timing and taste made it an instant success. For a couple of years he lived the high life—plenty of money, local prestige, and what seemed like a bright future.

At the restaurant, Rick met his future wife. Within six months they were married. In another six months they were expecting their first child.

In the meantime, business was slowing down. Construction along the road where his restaurant was located made it difficult to park, so many patrons stayed away. Others flocked to the hot spots du jour. While business didn't grind to a halt, the restaurant was still losing money at a pace that was getting dangerous. In addition, Rick and his wife both agreed that the hours required of him to run a restaurant would give them no time to be together with the new baby.

Reluctantly, Rick decided to close his business. He sold the restaurant but because of the debt it had incurred, he received very little cash. That left him with the prospect of starting over with nearly $50,000 in personal credit card debt he had racked up over the last year.

While Rick's extensive contacts quickly led to a good sales job, the pay wasn't enough to make a dent in the credit card bills. Wanting to avoid bankruptcy at all costs, he found a debt negotiation (or debt settlement) company that offered to negotiate settlements of his debts. Rick entered the program and in two years the credit card debts were all negotiated and paid off. By then he was earning a steady income and was able to start saving money for a down payment on a new home. They'd need a larger place, after all, with another child on the way.

Credit Card Companies Aren't Doing Too Badly . . .

Credit card giant MBNA reported that in 2003 its second quarter cardholder fee income increased 23.1 percent to $121.1 million, in part because of an increase in the average fees assessed, including higher late and overlimit fees. Credit card fees charged by MBNA include annual, late, overlimit, returned check, cash advance, express payment, and other miscellaneous fees on credit card loans. In 2003, MBNA made a profit of $2.34 billion.

American Express Company also reported record net income of $770 million for the third quarter, up 12 percent from the year before.

According to the nonprofit Consumer Action, more than one third of surveyed issuers said they will raise existing cardholders' rates because of their poor credit record with other creditors—even if the cardholder has made no late payments or other missteps with the card in question.

Consumer Action has also found that the number of issuers with $35 late fees doubled between 2002 and 2003.

Debt Elimination

Have you seen the ads arguing that our credit/banking system is illegal? The ads claiming that because of this illegality you can wipe out all your debts? Are you tempted?

Bernice and Bill were having money troubles. They were feeding their children but were falling behind on the mortgage. Bill drove a big rig and with gas prices up and freight hauling down he was having difficulty making ends meet.

Bernice's mother, Gladys, was saddened by this situation. She had always wanted the best for her daughter and grandchildren. Gladys tried to get money to Bernice to help when she could. But Gladys was living close to the edge on a monthly basis herself and couldn't afford to consistently bail out Bernice and Bill.

Bill's father, George, was also troubled by the problems. But rather than give money George sought to give advice. He suggested that Bill find someone to live in the house who could make the payments. Bill and family could move into a cheaper place they could afford, the renter of Bill's existing house could pay the mortgage, and in a few years when Bill was in a better financial condition he could move back into the house and not lose the equity he was building in it.

Bill was not in the mood to take anyone's money or anyone's advice. He was angry at himself but more and more he was angry at the system.

He was angry that the taxes he paid were squandered on lazy workers and stupid programs. He was angry at the oil companies for their price manipulation. He was angry that the payroll taxes he had to pay went for Social Security and Medicare. The entire country knew they would never receive the benefit of that money, so why did everyone keep blindly paying into the system?

More and more Bill believed the system was stacked against him. And then Joe, a friend at work, told him about debt elimination.

Joe indicated there were a number of sites on the Internet that told the truth about America's banking system. By doing a search under the headings "Debt Elimination" or "Mortgage Elimination," Joe said he would find the sites where the dark truths would be revealed.

Bill spent several hours on the Internet learning what he knew in his heart. The American banking system was a fraud. It created money out of thin air.

At one site, Sentinel Counselors for American Mortgages, Bill learned that he didn't have to pay his mortgage. This was because his mortgage was not a loan but an exchange. Bill had given the bank a promissory note to pay $100,000. The bank deposited that as an asset. Thus, the bank owes him $100,000 because they are treating Bill's promise to pay as an asset by their own bookkeeping.

Bill was very excited by this information and told Bernice triumphantly that they didn't have to pay their mortgage.

Bernice was confused. The $100,000 they borrowed went to the previous owners for his property. How could they get out of paying that?

Because, Bill argued, the bank had never created a loan. Their promissory note was a bookkeeping entry that allowed the bank to create the appearance of a loan. But in fact no true money had been used. It was all pretend.

Bernice still didn't understand. Even if their promissory note was all pretend for accounting purposes, they had received an actual house in return. It had three bedrooms, two baths, and a nice kitchen. It wasn't pretend to her.

Bill became agitated. He said it was usury to pay interest on pretend loans, loans created out of thin air. The loan he had entered into did not involve monies backed by gold or silver or something real. The loan was instead propped up by people's valueless and worthless faith in the system.

Bernice was still confused. If people had faith in the system didn't that in and of itself create value? If everyone agrees to pay back what they borrow doesn't everyone benefit by being able to borrow?

Bill became very angry at her lack of understanding of the manipulative system that made people slaves to America's banks. He returned to the Sentinel Counselors for American Mortgages Web site to sign up for their debt elimination program. By paying $1,500 he would have the exclusive use of a counselor trained in debt elimination. They would show him how to fill out the forms necessary to eliminate his debt.

The counselor on the phone congratulated Bill on his decision and reiterated that no legitimate debt had been created. The bank took his promise to pay $100,000 and made it into an asset—an asset the bank had to repay. Since there was no loan created but only an exchange with the bank, the forms he filled out would negate the exchange and free him from false debt.

After their first mortgage payment went unpaid, Bernice got a call from the bank. The mortgage was overdue and they needed to make a payment. Bernice mumbled an excuse, then immediately told Bill.

Bill told Bernice not to worry. He was in the process of eliminating the debt.

Bernice started sobbing. Why had he done that? It didn't make sense to begin with and now they were going to lose their home.

Bill raised his voice. They were not going to lose their home. Once the paperwork was processed the mortgage would be canceled and the debt eliminated. America's fraudulent bankers would be off their backs.

Bernice pleaded with him. How could they possibly receive their $100,000 home for free? It wasn't fair or right to use some convoluted argument to get out of an obligation they had freely entered into two years ago. She didn't want the house if they were going to cheat people out of it.

Bill shouted they were going to own the house without fraudulent debt and stormed out. He had a long haul to make and was already late.

When he returned Bernice was preparing to move. The bank was threatening to foreclose and Bernice had no money of her own to make the payments. She told Bill he could pack his own things. They would be living in different places.

Bill was furious. He called the debt elimination company demanding to know why his debt wasn't eliminated.

The representative on the phone was glib. The debt was already eliminated because it never existed at the start.

Then why, Bill demanded, was he losing his house?

The representative calmly explained that the banking system illegally maintained improper control of the courts and the legal system. While the debt was not real the banks had the ability to enforce their fraud through the corrupt use of legal power.

Bill was angry. That was a nice smooth answer, he fumed, but it didn't get him his house back. He had paid $1,500 to have the debt eliminated. He didn't want excuses.

The representative insisted that they had no control over the court system. They only assisted with the necessary paperwork. Dealing with the corrupt use of power and illegal taking of homes was beyond the scope of their services.

Bill demanded his $1,500 back. The representative said that was impossible. They had helped him fill out the two one-page forms. Sentinel Counselors for American Mortgages had earned their fee.

Bill was now distraught. He had lost his wife and was about to lose his home. He called his father and told him the whole story.

While supportive and calming, George said he should have known the outcome from the start.

Bill wanted to know why.

His father asked him to repeat the company name and pointed out their acronym: SCAM.

The lesson of this story is to stay away from debt elimination and mortgage elimination programs. The only help they provide is to help themselves to your money and help you get into deeper trouble.

Bankruptcy

The word bankruptcy alone can conjure a range of emotions including shame, disapproval, and fear. If you've been through a bankruptcy, you may wish it never happened. If you haven't ever had to file, you may judge those who have as simply irresponsible with their finances. The truth is, common life events such as divorce, a small business that goes under, a lawsuit, or an unexpected illness can throw anyone's financial life into a tailspin and land them in bankruptcy court.

According to bankruptcy researcher Harvard Law professor Elizabeth Warren, in her book *The Two-Income Trap*, nobody is immune from the possibility of bankruptcy. Bankruptcy occurs in all walks of life and income levels. "The data show that families filing for bankruptcy last year were a cross section of middle-class America," she says. Warren has reported bankrupt debtors to be:

- At an educational level slightly higher than average in the U.S.
- About a 50/50 mix of homeowners and renters.
- Employed in fields that mirror the range of occupations in the U.S. job market.

In addition:

- About 90 percent would be classified as "solidly middle-class."
- Two out of three debtors had lost a job at some point shortly before filing.
- Nearly half had medical problems.
- One fifth of the debtors had recently been through a divorce.

Professor Warren points out that jobs, medical problems, and divorce account for about 80 percent of the filings.

Her scariest statistic, however, is this: The single greatest predictor that a woman will file bankruptcy is whether she has children. If current trends continue, one in seven middle-class families will declare bankruptcy by the end of the decade.

What Happens in Bankruptcy Currently?

Currently, most people file under Chapter 7 of the bankruptcy code. This is often called "straight bankruptcy." In a Chapter 7 filing, some or all debts are discharged (or written off). In exchange, the debtor may lose property that was not "exempt" from bankruptcy.

The process usually takes some thirty to ninety days, and after it's completed, debtors can begin to rebuild their financial lives. While these consumers will pay higher rates for credit, and find it more difficult to reestablish credit, they are able to start over again when their bankruptcies are completed.

A much smaller percentage of consumers file under Chapter 13 of the bankruptcy code. This is often called a "wage earner's plan." In a Chapter 13 filing, the consumer agrees to pay back a portion of his or her debts under a court-ordered plan administered by a bankruptcy trustee. Chapter 13 is chosen when a consumer wants to make a good-faith effort to pay back debts, when he or she doesn't qualify for a Chapter 7, or because there are some assets the debtor wants to keep but would lose under a Chapter 7 plan.

Debtors typically are not able to begin rebuilding their credit until the bankruptcy plan is completed, but there is a bright side: Chapter 13 bankruptcies are voluntarily removed from credit reports seven years after filing, while Chapter 7 bankruptcies are reported for ten years from filing.

A few things to understand about bankruptcy:

• Bankruptcy can stop collection efforts, giving you time to deal with your debts. But even a Chapter 7 won't erase all debts. For example, you'll still have to deal with student loan payments, most tax debts, child support, and spousal support. While foreclosure may be postponed, you'll still have to be able to pay your mortgage and catch up on your payments if you want to keep your home. Your attorney can give you more details.

• You'll have to pay attorney's fees and filing fees, which can add up to a few thousand dollars. While some companies will offer to help you do it on your own, it's best to get an attorney if you can because it is getting increasingly difficult to file a Chapter 7.

• If you have co-signed debts and you file for bankruptcy but the other borrower doesn't, they will be on the hook for the entire debt.

If you think bankruptcy may become inevitable, it's better that you meet with an attorney sooner rather than later to discuss it. Many people make costly mistakes that they could have avoided if they understood the facts. One prime example: raiding retirement funds to pay bills, then ending up in bankruptcy anyway. Those retirement funds may have been protected from creditors.

Debtors Anonymous

Much like the Alcoholics Anonymous twelve-step program, Debtors Anonymous focuses on helping debtors to stop taking on debt. It can be a valuable resource for people who find themselves in debt again and again. See the Resources section.

Mental Health Help

According to a survey by Myvesta, almost half of people with problem debt can be classified as depressed. Of those, just under 40 percent reported symptoms of severe depression. In comparison, studies have shown that 9.5 percent of the general population are clinically depressed.

This means if you are struggling with debt you may first need to make an appointment with a mental health counselor or your doctor to try to get any clinical depression under control. It's pretty difficult to take charge of your financial life when just getting through the day is a challenge.

The Costly Mistake

The biggest mistake people make when they are deep in debt is to procrastinate. It's the "deer in the headlights" syndrome, and credit counselors and bankruptcy attorneys see it all the time. It's painfully obvious to everyone except the person in debt that they need to make a hard choice or they won't have many choices left.

The other response is what financial expert Steve Rhode calls "magical thinking." Americans by and large are an optimistic lot. We buy lottery tickets and spend tomorrow's income today, and well before the ship comes in. That can be a costly mistake when it comes to getting out of debt.

As Elizabeth Warren states in *The Two-Income Trap:* "The greatest danger for a family in financial distress is not bill collectors (although they can be the most annoying). The greatest danger is false optimism. We heard it over and over again in our interviews [for their study of bankruptcy]: 'We thought Mark would be back at work right away. . . . We didn't think Grandpa could go on like this much longer.' These families knew they had been hit by a disaster but they didn't respond fast enough because they thought it would pass quickly."

Don't let debt scare you into doing nothing. You know your options. Now get the help you need so you can focus your time and energy on creating a positive financial future.

Chapter VII

Emergency Measures for Special Debt Situations

Car Loan Troubles

Vehicles are expensive. According to Edmunds.com, the average new vehicle sticker price in 2003 was over $30,000, while the average cost consumers paid after rebates and negotiations was just over $26,000. Consumers are also stretching their payments out longer—an average of over 62 months, or just over five years. That sets a record for the average length of time for a vehicle loan.

What does this mean to you? It means that you, like many people, may be upside down on your car, owing more than it's worth. It means that if you do decide you want to get rid of your car you'll have no choice but to get into a more expensive loan, one that pays off the new car and the remaining balance of the old one.

It may also mean that the payments that were affordable when you took your loan may not be so easy to make now—especially if your income has gone down or if you've had expensive car repairs. And let's not forget the increasing price of a gallon of gas.

If you are having trouble keeping up with expensive car loan payments, here are several options to consider:

DIFFICULTY KEEPING UP YOUR PAYMENTS

Refinance it: Many people don't realize that car loans can be refinanced just like mortgages and other types of loans. The best time to refinance is *before* you fall behind. Even if you have less than perfect credit, though, you may be able to find a lender that will refinance you.

> ☞ *Credit Maximizer Tip:* Though multiple inquiries from auto lenders aren't supposed to hurt your credit score much (see Chapter 9), it's still possible they will, so shop carefully.

Sell it: If you're not upside down, meaning you owe less than your car is worth, you may just want to sell it and find something cheaper in the meantime. You're certainly better off doing this than having it repo'd and sold at an auction for far less than you'll likely get on your own. You may also be able to get the lender to agree to let a creditworthy borrower take over the loan but that may take some negotiating.

Work it out: If you've had your car loan for at least six months (and made those payments on time), your lender may be willing to work out a modified payment schedule for you. There are several ways they can do this, including letting you skip a payment or two and tack them onto the end of the loan, or allowing you to make smaller payments for a few months, then getting back on track. In some cases, the entire loan can be modified. It depends on your situation and the lender's policies. But you won't know if you don't ask.

It is essential that you get any agreements from your creditor *in writing*! And *don't assume anything*. You may assume, for example, that by agreeing to your lower payments, the lender won't report you as late to the credit bureaus. Your assumption may be wrong. (And when that late payment hits your credit report, credit card companies that you've been paying on time may hike your interest rates.) Be forewarned and negotiate as much as you can.

Turn it in: In a voluntary repossession, you turn in the car and save the lender the repossession costs. It can still be reported on your credit report (and will be considered seriously negative) but that may be negotiable too. Talk to your lender if this is your only option. If you show a hardship situation, they may be willing to work with you.

Get help: What if you can't work it out? Or if your income is unstable or low, and unlikely to pick up? If your car is vital for getting to your job, or getting the kids to school or child care, for example, you may want to focus on paying that loan first and letting other bills (like credit cards) slide until you can catch up. Or by using the advice in the previous chapter and working with a reputable counseling agency or debt settlement firm, you may be able to cut your other bills so you can keep up with the essential ones.

Bankruptcy may be another option. If you file, you may be able to keep your car without having to catch up on those payments that are behind right now. And in some situations you may be able to just pay off the current value of the car (as opposed to the full loan) as well as stretch out your payments. For more information, talk with a bankruptcy attorney.

VEHICLE REPOSSESSION

If you fall behind on your car loan or lease, the lender (or lessor) may have the right to repossess your vehicle. Each state has its own laws, but in many states repossession can happen quickly, without any advance notice or permission from the court. Plus, the lender may have the right to sell your loan contract to a third party, who can also repossess the vehicle if you fall behind or otherwise default on your contract.

There are some limits on repossessions, however, and if the lender violates these rules you may be entitled to damages.

FALLING BEHIND IN YOUR PAYMENTS

Many people mistakenly think that even if they fall behind on their car loan or lease, as long as they are paying something it can't be repossessed. They also may think that their car can't be repo'd unless they fall at least ninety days behind. That usually is not true.

The contract you signed when you took out the loan will spell out the definition of "default." Failing to pay on time once may put you in default. Letting your insurance lapse may do the same. In addition, the fact that you are in default may allow some lenders to "accelerate" your loan, or ask for the full balance immediately. In some states, lenders must notify you when you are in default and give you the opportunity to catch up before they can take your vehicle.

While lenders can usually go onto your property to take your car, they usually can't commit what's called a "breach of the peace." This may include:

- Removing your car from a closed or locked garage without your permission.
- Using physical threats or force to take your car.

It is often legal, however, for the repo man to:

- Come onto your property to take your car.
- Hotwire your car or use a duplicate key to take it.

If you had any items in the vehicle when it was taken, you're usually entitled to get them back. But you may have to claim them quickly (sometimes within twenty-four hours), so don't delay if your vehicle was repo'd and you had items of value inside.

Your state attorney general's office should be able to give you information about state vehicle repossession laws. Visit www.naag.org for a referral to your state attorney general's office. Lenders who breach the peace in seizing your car may be required to compensate you if they harm you or your property.

SELLING YOUR VEHICLE

When your car is repossessed, it will ordinarily be sold. While it is usually sold at a public auction, some states allow private sales as well. You always have the right to redeem your vehicle before it's sold by paying the full balance due plus any associated costs and fees. (Of course, if you could afford to do that it's unlikely you would have lost it in the first place!)

In other states, the law is more consumer-friendly. In those states, you can reinstate the loan if you can pay the amount you're behind plus late fees, repossession costs, and related expenses (such as attorney's fees). This too can be tough if you're already behind, but you may be able to work out a temporary arrangement with a friend or relative who can lend you the money to catch up. Of course you'll have to keep up with your payments then or risk losing your vehicle again.

If your car is sold, then whatever the sale brings, minus allowable expenses for repossessing and selling the car, will be applied toward your loan balance. These public auctions usually do not bring top dollar, so you'll likely be billed for the difference, or the deficiency. For example, say you owe $15,000 on your car, and it's sold at auction for $10,000 and there were $1,500 in costs for the repossession and sale, there would be a deficiency of $6,500.

If you can't pay the deficiency, the lender will likely turn that balance over to a collection agency or may sue to get a deficiency judgment. That means your headaches still aren't over when the vehicle is gone. You may well have no vehicle, a damaged credit record, and still be harassed for the balance.

On the other hand, if you really can't pay the deficiency and the lender decides it's not worth trying to collect, you may be sent a tax form 1099-C listing the deficiency amount as income. The IRS considers this "forgiven debt" income and will expect you to pay taxes on it unless you can show that you are insolvent. (See the section on taxes later in this chapter.)

If your car is sold, it must be sold in a "commercially reasonable manner." Again, that doesn't mean it has to be sold for top dollar, but it can't be sold for a rock-bottom price so that the seller can work out a side agreement and pocket the difference. Many auctioned vehicles are sold at dealer auctions and the dealers are going to bid a low enough price to be able to resell the vehicle and still make a profit.

If you think your repo'd vehicle may not have been sold in a commercially reasonable manner, it would be a good idea to talk with your state attorney general's office and a consumer law attorney in your area.

CO-SIGNERS BEWARE!

If you co-signed for a vehicle and the other borrower didn't pay, you'll face the same consequences as the original borrower. And in most cases, the lender doesn't even have to notify the co-signer that the loan is delinquent.

Example: John co-signed a loan for his father, who needed the vehicle to get to work. His father couldn't keep up on the payments when he fell ill, and the truck was repo'd. John didn't know about the problem with the truck, and his father died soon after.

Three years later, John started receiving collection calls about a $20,000 deficiency balance on the truck. He couldn't afford to pay it, but managed to keep the debt collectors at bay for a couple of years. Finally, he received a notice that the balance was reported to the IRS as "Discharge of Indebtedness Income" and he was forced to pay taxes as if he had received that $20,000 in income.

If you are being dunned for a vehicle you co-signed for, try to work out a reasonable settlement with the lender. (See the chapter on debt collectors for more advice.)

Mortgage Troubles

We've already discussed the pros and cons of using home equity to refinance other debt. But what if you already have a mortgage and are having trouble keeping up with the payments? This isn't unusual: Tens of thousands of Americans lose their homes to foreclosure each year.

If you're falling behind on your mortgage it's important to get a plan together quickly and act on it. It's easy to feel overwhelmed and afraid. But waiting too long can cost you your home.

Many good, hardworking, honest people lose their home to foreclosure and one of the main reasons is that they simply refuse to acknowledge that they are in trouble. They keep waiting or hoping for a solution to bail them out, and it doesn't. If you're in trouble, work on a solution now!

How the foreclosure works depends on which state you live in, and can take a very short time or as long as a year and a half.

If you do lose your home to foreclosure, and the foreclosing lender gets less than is owed (plus expenses) from the sale, there is a deficiency. For example, if you owed $100,000 on your mortgage and the lender incurred $7,000 in expenses foreclosing and selling the property, then received only $90,000 in the sale, there is a deficiency of $17,000. ($100,000 + $7,000 − $90,000). If there is a deficiency, you may face two nasty surprises:

1. The lender may have to report this "forgiven" amount to the IRS on a 1099-C, and you'll be expected to pay taxes on it as if it were income to you. If that's the case, make sure you talk with a tax advisor who may be able to help you wipe out that tax debt if you are insolvent.

2. The lender may sue you for the deficiency—the difference between what you owed plus expenses and what they received in the sale of the property. That means that you may still have a lender trying to collect from you even after the foreclosure.

If you had a second loan or other liens on the property, and the lender with the first mortgage forecloses, then those secondary loans or liens are usually wiped out in the foreclosure. The important exception is tax liens, which must be paid before the property can be sold again.

So it's often better to avoid foreclosure if you can. Here are some strategies:

STRATEGIES TO AVOID FORECLOSURE

Catch up on your payments: In some states, you can stop the foreclosure by paying the amount you are behind plus any other fees due. In some states, this does *not* stop the lender from foreclosing. Of course, if you could do this you might not be in trouble in the first place.

Sell: If the market is strong and you have enough equity in your home to pay the closing costs associated with a sale, you may be best off selling your home. The lender may even put your foreclosure on hold for a little longer to allow you to do that. Be sure to get any agreements from the lender to that effect in writing.

If you are behind on your payments, think twice about trying to sell your home "by owner" or with a part-time agent to save on the real estate commission. If you are pressed for time, your best bet is to get a full-time agent with an excellent track record who will price and market your home aggressively for a fast sale. Also watch out for real estate agents who throw out a high sales figure just to get your listing. You need to be realistic in your expectations, and get the house sold before you lose it.

Let someone take over your payments: If your payments are reasonable for the area, but you don't have enough equity to sell your home, you may be able to sell it to a buyer "subject to" the current mortgage. In other words, they take over your mortgage payments and then refinance the loan to pay you off at an agreed upon time in the future. You may also be able to get a little cash out of the deal to move to another place. This can keep you out of foreclosure and keep the mortgage in good standing.

There are two caveats here. First, most loans today are not assumable. That means you really can't allow someone to just assume (that is, take over) your mortgage. The loan contract usually contains an acceleration clause that allows the lender to call the entire loan due if they learn the house has been sold subject to the mortgage. As long as they are getting their monthly payments, most lenders won't enforce a due-on-sale clause, but you should be aware of the risk.

The second warning is of a *serious* risk. There are people who prey on homeowners in pre-foreclosure. They use a variety of tactics to essentially buy your home very cheaply. One of these schemes is equity skimming, in which the "buyer" offers to take care of your financial troubles by putting someone in your home. They will often have you deed the house over to them, then promise to make the mortgage payments. They collect rent but don't pay your mortgage so you end up in foreclosure anyway.

Another scheme is a fraudulent sale/leaseback arrangement where the investor agrees to buy your home and lease it back to you. You are promised that in a year or so your credit will be repaired and you'll be able to buy the home back. But the terms of the deal are usually so onerous that you end up losing the house—often at a ridiculously low price.

Working with an investor to keep you out of foreclosure isn't always a bad option. In some cases, it may be your best option for preventing your foreclosure. But since this is an emotional and complicated transaction, be careful. Choose an experienced investor to work with.

Rent it: If your monthly payment is attractive, you may be able to find a renter who can cover your payments while you work out your financial difficulties. This is risky for you, of course, because if the renter can't—or doesn't—pay, you'll be trying to evict them while scrambling to keep your home. If you consider this option, make sure you hire a company to do a full background check on your tenant, get a healthy deposit plus first and last month's rent, and consider using a management company to manage the property for a monthly fee.

Give it back: With a "deed in lieu of foreclosure," you save the lender time and money by avoiding the foreclosure process. Essentially you deed your house back to the lender. While a deed in lieu can be reported on your credit report (and can be a seriously negative mark), you may be able to negotiate with the lender not to report it. Keep in mind that if you have a second mortgage or home equity line of credit, deeding it back to the lender does *not* wipe out the second loan. Just because you don't have the home anymore does not mean the lenders cannot try to collect on the second.

Note: You will be asked on future mortgage loan applications whether you have ever transferred title back to a lender to avoid foreclosure, so even if it's not on your credit report, it may come up again.

Refinance it: If you have equity in your home, you may be able to refinance it out of pre-foreclosure. It can be tricky, though, and the last thing you want to do is waste your time with a mortgage lender or broker who promises you the world then can't get the loan. Also watch out for very high interest rates or prepayment penalties that will make it difficult to sell if you need to. When you're desperate to save your home, you may be willing to do just about anything, but predatory loans can make matters worse. Make sure you're dealing with a broker or lender who has actually helped consumers in trouble, and don't let them drag it out too long.

Short-sale it: If you owe close to what your home is worth—or more than it's worth—you may be able to get the lenders to agree to a short sale. You'll need a buyer for your home (no, it cannot be a relative!) and this is probably best done with an investor who already has successfully done short sales, simply because they'll know how to negotiate with the lender.

Example: Let's say your home is worth around $80,000 and you owe about $75,000. Even if you sold if for the full $80,000, your closing costs and real estate commissions would put you in the hole—which you can't afford since you're already behind. In addition, if you've fallen behind on your mortgage, you've probably put off repairs and the house probably isn't in tip-top condition.

A savvy real estate investor may work out a deal with the bank to pay them off at $65,000 and give you a little money to help you move. The bank gets more than they probably would in a foreclosure, and you avoid a foreclosure (and avoid a possible deficiency judgment) and head to your new place.

Work it out: The lender may agree to modify your loan to allow you to catch up. Some of the modifications that can be worked out include:

- Tack the payments you are behind onto the end of the loan.
- Allow you to catch up on the missed payments by adding them to your current payments for a few months.
- Allow you to pay only interest, plus any escrows for taxes and insurance for a period of time.
- Reduce your interest rate and penalties.

Understand that the lender is going to want to see details of your financial situation both to support the fact that you are in a hardship situation, as well as to show that you will be able to get caught up and pay in the future. A workout would *not* be a realistic option, for example, if you have taken a significant cut in pay and have not secured extra income that would allow you to keep up with your bills.

File bankruptcy: Filing bankruptcy can stall a foreclosure, but it does *not* wipe out your mortgage debt. Depending on your state's laws, how far you are behind and what type of bankruptcy you file, you'll still have to be able to work out a payment arrangement to catch up on your mortgage and then continue to make your payments going forward. Sometimes, however, the stall is what you need to be able to sell your house or get an investor to buy it in a short sale situation (the court's permission will be required). In other situations, a bankruptcy can wipe out other debts making it possible for you to keep up with the mortgage payment.

Student Loan Woes

Today's students need to graduate with degrees in debt management. Consider these statistics from Consolidated Credit Counseling Services:

- 83 percent of undergraduate students have at least one credit card.
- 41 percent of students carry credit card debt with an average balance of $3,071.
- 39 percent of students now graduate with unmanageable student loan debt.
- A third of college seniors graduate with $20,000 or more in student loan debt.
- Just over half of students who used loans to pay for college say they feel burdened by their debt.
- 73 percent of parents of graduating seniors said they expect their son or daughter to take a job at a salary that would require some sort of financial boost from them. Within that group, 38 percent said their child might have to move back home with them.
- Only 44 percent of college students clearly understand the term budget.

While credit card debt among students is a growing problem, it's often tiny compared to the problem of student loan debt. Higher education costs are now so high that many students have no choice but to borrow. And they often borrow as much as they can, assuming that they'll have no trouble paying the loan back when they start working and earning a salary.

Many students (and their parents) also assume a higher education will "pay off" with a higher salary or perks, regardless of the field they are entering. It's not unusual for would-be schoolteachers or social workers, for example, to graduate with student loan debt of $30,000 or more.

Falling behind on a student loan can be expensive. The collection costs can be high, in addition to the interest you may already be paying. There is no statute of limitations for collecting most student loan debts. Unlike other debts where collectors have only a certain number of years to sue you, student loan debts can haunt you for years and years. Also, it is difficult to discharge most student loans in bankruptcy.

In addition, you will have trouble getting student loans in the future, your income tax refund may be seized, you may be subject to wage garnishment without first being taken to court, and you will find it difficult to catch up as well as pay off that student loan debt in the future.

However, there is some good news. If you are in default and enter a loan rehabilitation program, then make twelve consecutive on-time payments (note, you can't be one day late on those payments!), you can bring your loan out of default. When you do, your previous late payments will be removed from your credit report. Another option for getting out of default is to find out whether it is possible to consolidate your student loan out of default. See the Resources section for more information.

☞ *Credit Maximizer Tip:* If you have complaints about how your Direct Loans, FFEL Loans, Guaranteed Student Loans, and Perkins Loans have been handled, and cannot resolve the problem with the lender, contact the Department of Education's Student Loan Ombudsman Office at (877) 557-2575.

Here are some additional strategies for coping with high levels of student loan debt:

CANCELLATION
Student loans may be canceled in part or in full for any of the following:

• Total and permanent disability. Loans may be discharged if a doctor certifies that you are totally and permanently disabled and unable to work or earn money.

• School closure. If you received a student loan at a school that closed before you completed your studies, you may be eligible for discharge of your loan.

• Ability to benefit. Your loan can be discharged if the school admitted you based on your ability to benefit from the training but you weren't properly tested to measure that ability or you failed the test.

- Child and family services cancellation. You may be eligible to cancel your student loan if you are solely "providing or supervising the provision of services to high-risk children who are from low-income communities and the families of those children."

- Teacher cancellation discharge. You may be eligible to cancel your student loan if you are teaching full-time at a low-income school, as determined by your state's education agency; are a special education teacher, including teacher of infants, toddlers, children, or youths with disabilities; or teach in the fields of mathematics, science, foreign languages, or bilingual education, or in any other field of expertise determined by a state education agency to have a shortage of qualified teachers in that state.

- Forged signature. If someone forged your signature on the loan application, promissory note, or authorization for electronic funds transfer, you may qualify for a loan discharge.

- School owes you a refund. You may also qualify for partial discharge of an FFEL or Direct Loan if your school failed to pay a tuition refund required under federal law.

- Death. If you die with an outstanding student loan, your federal student loan debt will be discharged. Your estate will not owe any money on your loan.

DEFERMENT AND FORBEARANCE

Deferment: Deferment allows you to temporarily postpone payments on your loan. If you have a subsidized loan, including Perkins Loans, interest won't be charged during the deferment. If your loan is unsubsidized, you will be responsible for the interest on the loan during the deferment.

Forbearance: If you are temporarily unable to meet your repayment schedule but are not eligible for a deferment, you may receive forbearance for a limited and specified period. During forbearance, your payments are postponed or reduced. Whether your loans are subsidized or unsubsidized, you will be charged interest. Forbearance may be available because you are:

- Unable to pay due to poor health or other unforeseen personal problems.

- Serving in a medical or dental internship or residency.
- Making federal student loan payments that are equal to or greater than 20 percent of your monthly gross income.

It is important that you contact your lender about deferment or forbearance *before* you fall behind on your payments. If you wait until you are behind, you may not be eligible. Continue making your payments until your deferment or forbearance is approved.

In addition, the fact that you are in a forbearance or deferment arrangement may be reported on your credit report and may be considered negative. It may, however, keep you out of default, which can be very expensive and will be worse for your credit rating.

OTHER OPTIONS

Graduated repayment plan: With one of these plans, your payments start out low and will rise over time. This plan is often good for a student who is just starting out and expects their salary to increase as they gain more experience. Caution: One of these plans can stretch your loan out to as long as thirty years.

Extended repayment plan: An extended repayment plan allows you to pay your student loan over twelve to thirty years instead of the standard ten years. It is more expensive, but if the lower payments keep you out of default, it should be worth it.

Income contingent plan: With one of these plans, your payment is based on your adjusted gross income (AGI)—as reported on your U.S. income tax return—your family size, the interest rate, and the total amount of your Direct Loan debt.

Consolidation: If you have more than one student loan, you may be able to consolidate them into a lower-cost single-payment loan. This can save you money if the new payment is lower than your previous combined payment, which is often the case because it is a new loan. Your consolidated student loan payment is based on the average interest rate on the student loans you are consolidating. Your consolidated rate is set by the government. So, there is not a whole lot of advantage in shopping around among different lenders.

In some cases, consolidating your student loan can also take you out of default, which can benefit you in a couple of ways. One way, of course, is by halting the collection costs associated with a defaulted student loan. The other way it can benefit you is that it can help your credit report. If you make twelve consecutive on-time payments on a student loan that you have brought out of default, the previous late payments can be erased. For more information on consolidating student loans, see the Resources section.

BE A SMART BORROWER

It's not unusual for student loans to be sold, or for a student to have eight or more loans! It can be tough keeping track of them all. Lose track of a loan, though, and you may quickly find yourself in student loan hell. The Department of Education offers these tips for being a smart borrower, and they're good ones:

- **Keep all your loan documents.** This simple piece of advice is one of the most important. You'll have problems later if you can't find your promissory note, can't remember what type of loans you received, or don't know who you're supposed to repay or how you go about postponing (deferring) repayment if you have financial difficulties. Keep a file of all documents connected with your loans from the time you first get a loan, so you'll always have what you need in one place. Then you won't be confused about what you're supposed to do or who you're supposed to contact if you have questions.
- **Keep records.** Whenever you talk to your lender or loan servicer, keep a record of the person you talked to, the date you had the conversation, and what was said. If you send letters, always include your loan account number, and keep copies of those letters (and the responses you receive) in your file. That way, you'll know who said what and when, which can help you avoid problems and misunderstandings.
- **Notify your school and/or loan holder in writing.** If you move, change your name or Social Security number, or reenroll in school, you must make sure your loan holder won't lose track of you. If that happens, you could miss payments and become delinquent (late). Also, your loan could be sold, and you won't know who has it or where to send payments because you couldn't be notified.

- **Ask questions.** If there's something you don't understand or if you're having trouble making payments—ask. Don't wait until things become too tough—ask for help from your loan holder or loan servicer right away!

When You Owe Taxes

Of any debt, tax debt is perhaps the most stressful. The IRS can be very aggressive in its collection efforts, and has strong, some may say extreme, powers that mere lenders don't, such as placing a lien on your property (or even seizing it), garnishing your wages, or seizing money from your bank account, all without going to court first. Tax liens are the only debt to remain on your credit report *forever* if they are not paid. If paid, they still remain on your report for seven years from the date they are paid.

If you owe the IRS money, whether it's a recent debt or one that's years old, it's time to figure out a way to settle up. Here are some options to consider:

Tap your savings: If you have money stashed away to pay the bill, do it. If you have some money saved but not enough for the entire bill, read the sections below on repayment plans and offers in compromise.

Repayment plan: You can ask the IRS for a repayment plan if you don't currently have an installment agreement in place and you have filed all required federal tax returns. You file Form 9645 and request an affordable payment plan. If the IRS approves your plan, you'll pay a $43 fee plus interest. The interest rate is reasonable.

If your request is approved, you'll be able to pay your taxes in monthly payments instead of immediately paying the amount in full. In return, you'll need to make your monthly payments on time, and pay all your current and future tax liabilities. (That means you shouldn't adjust your withholdings so high that you'll end up with another tax bill you can't pay!)

Charge Them: You can pay your taxes with a credit card at www.officialpayments.com. The service charges a fee of 2.49 percent, plus you'll pay interest on your credit card at the credit card companies' rate. It may not always be the cheapest way to go, but it can be better than letting IRS interest and penalties continue to accrue.

Offer in compromise: An offer in compromise is an agreement between a taxpayer and the IRS that resolves the taxpayer's tax debt. The IRS has the authority to settle, or "compromise," federal tax liabilities by accepting less than full payment under certain circumstances. It's considered a "last resort," but the IRS may be willing to accept an offer in compromise if there is:

- Doubt that the assessed tax is correct.
- Doubt that you could ever pay the full amount of tax owed.
- Extenuating circumstances such that the collection of the tax would create an economic hardship or would be unfair and inequitable.

You don't need a tax professional to prepare an offer in compromise, but it may be helpful depending on your circumstances.

File bankruptcy: Bankruptcy generally does not wipe out tax debts, but there are situations where it can be used to eliminate older tax bills. Consult a bankruptcy attorney for advice. As I've mentioned elsewhere, it may eliminate other bills so you are able to pay off your tax debt and other essential bills.

☞ *Credit Maximizer Tip:* If you have "fudged" things on your taxes, or have some questionable issues, hire a tax attorney to help you. CPAs and enrolled agents may be called to testify against you in tax court, but your communications with tax attorneys are protected by attorney client privilege.

Forgiven debt: If you settle a debt for less than you owe, or if the creditor writes it off, the lender may send the IRS a 1099-C which is used to report "discharge of indebtedness income." In fact, creditors are required to do this if the forgiven debt exceeds $600. You normally will be sent a copy of this too, but if you've moved it may not reach you. The IRS expects you to pay taxes on this "income." If, however, you can show the IRS you are insolvent before the debt was written off, you may be able to get out of paying that tax. Request Form 982 plus instructions from the IRS if you want to take this approach.

Military Matters: The Service Members Civil Relief Act (formerly the Soldiers' and Sailors' Relief Act of 1940)

The plight of military personnel and their bills is nothing new. As early in our country's history as the Civil War, American servicemen were faced with trying to handle civil matters while simultaneously serving their country. In an effort to protect the interests of the nation while protecting those of Northern servicemen, Congress passed a moratorium on civil actions brought against Union sailors and soldiers. The moratorium recognized that military personnel need to be able to concentrate on the work of fighting a war rather than worrying about bills back home. At the same time, the moratorium recognized that military personnel were not always paid enough to take care of the bills that stacked up while they were away serving the needs of the country. In simplest terms, the moratorium established that any civil actions (breach of contract, bankruptcy, foreclosure, divorce proceedings, and the like) brought against a serviceman were deferred until he returned home.

In 1918, the moratorium was brought back into effect for military personnel serving in World War I. The Soldiers' and Sailors' Civil Relief Act of 1918 was not as comprehensive as the Civil War moratorium, but it did protect active service members from bankruptcy, repossession of property, foreclosure, and similar actions. After World War I, the act expired.

The Soldiers' and Sailors' Civil Relief Act of 1940 took the act of 1918 one step further by lifting the setting of an expiration date for the soldiers serving in World War II. Between 1918 and 2003, the act was amended eleven times to reflect military and societal changes.

On December 19, 2003, President Bush replaced the law by signing into effect the Service Members Civil Relief Act (SCRA). The new act retains the intent of the 1918 and 1940 acts, while also taking into account the changes our world has seen in the years since.

The SCRA helps service personnel meet their legal and financial obligations while fulfilling their military duties. It is not meant to help servicemen and women ignore their obligations, but rather it is meant to ease their burdens during active service. For example, the SCRA allows service personnel to cancel vehicle leases if they are deployed for 180 days or more. After all, they won't be using the vehicle; is it right that they be required to pay?

Similarly, servicemen and women with permanent change-of-station orders or who are deployed to a new location for ninety days or more have the right to terminate housing leases. Nor can a member of the service or his or her family be evicted from housing while the service member is on active duty unless certain conditions are met (such as a court order or lease rents in excess of $2,400, among others).

The SCRA offers service personnel an automatic ninety-day stay in all judicial and administrative civil proceedings upon application. Additional stays may be requested as well. If an additional stay is denied, the court must appoint counsel to protect the rights of the serviceman or woman while he or she is on active duty.

The SCRA includes a 6 percent limit on interest rates for pre-service debts (including credit card debt). Any portion above 6 percent is not deferred, but permanently forgiven. After the service is complete, the serviceman or woman's monthly payments must reflect the amount of interest saved during the service period.

Service personnel in the Reserves are also protected under the SCRA from the time of their receipt of mobilization orders. This is meant to give them time to get their affairs in order.

Any serviceman or woman who claims the rights ensured under the SCRA is also protected from discrimination for such claims. You can't be fired from your job or evicted from your house or denied credit because you apply for SCRA coverage.

In addition to service personnel, the SCRA extends protection to Untied States citizens serving with allied forces in capacities considered similar to military service. The act also extends protection to dependents of service personnel if their ability to comply is materially effected by the serviceman or woman's military service.

The SCRA offers a variety of provisions to protect servicemen and women called to active service or long-term deployment. Most protections require a show of material effect as a prerequisite. Any member of the service facing either of these situations should check with their unit judge advocate or installation legal assistance officer for more information and assistance.

Chapter VIII

Debt Collectors

Debt collectors are in the business of doing one thing: collecting money. Often feared and dreaded, they can be aggressive and make your life stressful. Knowing your rights when it comes to debt collectors, though, can relieve some of that stress and help you take care of those annoying accounts.

There is a federal law called the Fair Debt Collection Practices Act (FDCPA) that requires that debt collectors treat you fairly. It doesn't stop them from trying to collect, but it does place certain limits on how they can collect.

The FDCPA applies to personal, family, and household debts. Business debts are not covered by the FDCPA. But if you used a personal credit card for purchases that were used by your business, the collector probably won't know that and is likely to follow the FDCPA if you know your rights.

A debt collector is any person who regularly collects debts owed to others. This includes attorneys who collect debts on a regular basis. It generally only applies to outside debt collection agencies, and not to creditors collecting their own debts, though your state may have laws that apply to creditors.

When you are first contacted by a debt collector, you should do several things:

1. Get contact information for the debt collector, including a phone number and address.

2. Dispute the debt if you think it's incorrect. Write to the collection agency immediately disputing the debt and requesting verification. Send your letter certified mail, return receipt requested. *You're entitled to this verification under the FDCPA.* Unless you are certain that you owe the full debt, disputing it will place the debt under dispute and give you time to figure out your options.

3. Start a correspondence file to keep notes about all your contacts with the collection agency: who called, what they said, and what was agreed. Also keep copies of all written correspondence. If the collector acts improperly, you may have legal remedies.

4. Verify that the statute of limitations for collecting the debt has not expired; for a state-by-state listing of collection time limits visit www.success dna.com. If it has, the collector can't sue you for the debt. And if you tell them to stop contacting you about the debt, they must comply (see below).

5. Do *not* pay a collector anything until you have established the debt is legitimate and worked out a payment arrangement. Don't be bullied!

Notification

Within five days after you are first contacted about a debt, the collector must send you a written notice telling you the amount of money you owe; the name of the creditor to whom you owe the money; and what to do if you dispute the debt.

Each state has laws that describe how long creditors or collection agencies can sue to collect various types of debts. These are called statutes of limitations. In some states, for some types of debts, it can be as little as four years, while in others it can be twenty years or more. This is important information because it's not unusual for collection agencies to make a last-ditch effort to try to collect a debt right before the statute of limitations expires.

Note: If you make a payment on a debt, it may extend or revive the statute of limitations. Let's say a collector contacts you about a ten-year-old debt that was outside the statute of limitations. They can't sue you to collect and they can't report it to the credit bureaus. So there's not a lot they can do to collect, especially if you tell them to leave you alone (see below). But if you pay them—even a token payment—it may start the statute of limitations over again!

It's also important to understand that paying a collection agency something, even a token payment, does *not* stop them from taking legal action to collect the debt. Collectors may pressure you to pay something to show "good faith." If you really can't afford to pay the debt or if you believe the debt is incorrect, you may be better off just refusing and asking them to leave you alone until you can repay. Making a payment—even a small one—may extend the statute of limitations.

Calling You

A collector may contact you in person, by mail, telephone, telegram, or fax. However, a debt collector may not contact you at inconvenient times or places, such as before 8:00 A.M. or after 9:00 P.M. your time, unless you say that's okay. A debt collector also may not contact you at work if the collector knows that your employer disapproves of such contacts. If you tell a collector that you're not allowed to take calls at work, make a note of that conversation. If they do it again, call an attorney.

Privacy

Collectors are not supposed to tell anyone who is not a co-signer on your debt about it, other than your spouse. They can call neighbors or employers to get your contact information, but that's about as far as they are allowed to go. They're not allowed to say that they are calling regarding a debt. If you hire an attorney to represent you, they should contact your attorney, not you.

Harassment, False Statements, and Unfair Practices

Anyone who has dealt with debt collectors for a while will discover that it's not unusual for them to lie and say just about anything to get you to pay.

There are legal limits on what they can say and do, but most people don't know their rights and so they just put up with it.

Watch out for any of the following types of statements or actions by collectors. Keep notes. If it looks like they are illegally harassing you, making false statements, or engaging in unfair practices, contact a consumer law attorney for help.

Examples of harassment:

- Threats of violence or harm.
- Obscene or profane language.
- Repeatedly using the telephone to annoy you.

Examples of false statements:

- Falsely implying that you have committed a crime, or that you will be arrested if you don't pay your debt.
- Falsely representing that they operate or work for a credit bureau.
- Misrepresenting the amount of your debt.
- Indicating that papers being sent to you are legal forms when they are not.
- Indicating that papers being sent to you are not legal forms when they are.
- Falsely implying that someone not responsible for the debt (usually a spouse or family member) will be responsible.
- Threatening action that they cannot take (garnishing your wages immediately without taking you to court, for example).

Important: A collector may threaten to notify your employer and garnish your wages if you don't pay immediately. For almost every type of consumer debt (except taxes and some student loans) the collector or creditor must first take you to court and get a judgment, *then* get the court's permission to garnish your wages. Whether they will actually go to those lengths depends on a number of things including how much you owe and how likely they think they are to collect. But it's not something that can generally happen overnight. Be alert to false statements like that from collectors and write them down.

Debt collectors may not engage in unfair practices when they try to collect a debt. For example, collectors may not:

- Collect any amount greater than your debt, unless allowed by state law.
- Deposit a postdated check prematurely.
- Take or threaten to take your property unless this can be done legally.
- Contact you by postcard.

Never, *ever* send a postdated check to a debt collector. If you knowingly bounce a check you can be subject to criminal penalties.

How to Stop a Debt Collector

If you send a letter to a debt collector asking them to stop contacting you, they must stop. But it won't stop them from taking legal action to collect the debt. You can still be sued for collection of the debt. It may make sense to write a "cease and desist" letter (just a fancy name for a letter telling them to leave you alone) if:

- You believe the statute of limitations has expired (point that out in your letter).
- You truly don't have the money to pay it (include a succinct description of your hardship situation).
- The debt collector is pressuring you to the point of creating unhealthy stress or physical side effects.
- You really don't believe you owe the debt and figure a judge would side with you if it ends up in court (describe why you believe you don't owe the debt).

See Appendix B for a sample cease and desist letter.

Negotiating

Collection accounts can often be negotiated for pennies on the dollar, especially if you can come up with a lump sum payment quickly. Most people are uncomfortable with negotiating but it's one of the most important skills you can learn and hone. I recommend you start your negotiations about 25 cents on the dollar. The debt collector may insist that there is a minimum amount they can accept, and that may or may not be true. You don't know. So you have to negotiate just as hard as they do.

It's much easier for debt collectors to try to get you to pay more than for you to pressure them to take less because:

1. The more they collect, the more they are likely to be paid, so it affects their bottom line,

2. It's not as emotional for them as it is for you, and

3. They negotiate debts every day, you don't.

Two other things to keep in mind:

1. Don't agree to something you can't afford. If you can't afford what they are proposing, tell the debt collector you can't and state that you'll call back when you've pulled some more money together. If they start threatening you, keep written notes and tell them you'll call back at another time.

2. Always try to get them to agree to remove any negative items from your credit report in exchange for payment. If they agree, you must get that in writing first, *before* you pay. Note that just listing a collection account as "paid" on your credit report is unlikely to raise your score.

There are companies that will do this negotiating for you if you're too uncomfortable. See the Resources section.

Scared and Pressured

If you are being pressured by debt collectors and are scared of what they can do if you don't pay, it may be worthwhile to talk with a consumer law attorney about your rights. The first consultation is usually free, but be sure to ask. Visit www.naca.net for a referral. If you can't afford a lawyer, call your local bar association and ask about legal services programs in your area that may be able to help.

Get Help

If you think the collector may be violating the law, get help from a consumer law attorney with experience in the FDCPA. You have the right to sue a collector in a state or federal court within one year from the date the law was violated. If you win, you may recover money for the damages you suffered plus an additional amount up to $1,000. Court costs and attorney's fees also can be recovered. A group of people also may sue a debt collector and recover money for damages up to $500,000, or one percent of the collector's net worth, whichever is less.

Report It

Report any problems you have with a debt collector to your state attorney general's office (go to www.naag.org and click on your state's listing) and the Federal Trade Commission (www.ftc.gov). The FTC receives significant numbers of complaints about collection agencies each year and reports those to Congress. While they don't get involved in individual disputes, they may take action against a collection company when they see a pattern of violations. Speak up!

Chapter IX

Credit Scores: Do You Rate?

When Robert Kiyosaki failed an English class in high school, his rich dad reminded him that his banker had never asked for his report card. His point wasn't that education is not important, but that your grades in school won't determine how much wealth you build over your lifetime.

There is a report card, though, that's much more important to your financial life than one you receive in school. And that's your credit report. Instead of As or Ds, your grade on that credit report will be a number: your credit score.

Your credit reports and scores play a strong role in:

- How much you pay for credit cards, mortgages, auto loans, and even some business loans.
- Whether you're able to borrow (hopefully for good debt) when you need to.
- The rates you pay for your auto or homeowner's insurance,
- How easy it is to get utility services, cell phone accounts, and many other services.

In this chapter and the next three, I am going to explain how credit reports and credit scores work, your rights, and most importantly how to maximize your credit to get the best deals.

If you have bad credit, don't get discouraged. You can get to work improving it as soon as you've read this book. And a poor credit rating doesn't have to stop your efforts to build wealth in their tracks. You may just have to be a little more creative.

If you want to buy real estate, for example, you can look for "hard money" loans, where the value of the property is what matters, not your credit. If you are starting a business, you can search out partners or shoestring it while you improve your credit. In other words, work on your credit, but don't let your credit stop you from reaching your goals!

Also, think for yourself, and don't be swayed by fair-weather friends . . .

When Charity Borders on Insanity

Donna was everyone's friend. She was the one who could be counted on to help a friend in need, be it moving into a new place, a late-night trip to the emergency room, or lending a few dollars here and there until payday.

Donna valued her circle of friends. They were important to her. She wasn't married and didn't have any family in the area. She enjoyed her friends' company and they enjoyed hers.

Donna did the books for a painting contractor. She was saving every month toward buying a house. She wanted her own cozy little home in the worst way. She wasn't sure she would ever get married and wanted at least the security of a place to call her own.

Then Lars came to work in the business. He was a tall, distinguished-looking man in his late forties. He was hired as a business development executive for the contractor owners, who wanted to line up more jobs with government agencies and larger businesses. Lars was a good salesman and he took a liking to Donna. She enjoyed the attention.

One evening over dinner, Lars asked Donna if he could discuss a car problem he was having. Always ready to lend an ear and help wherever needed, Donna urged that he discuss the problem.

Lars explained that he was looking to purchase a new Dodge Durango. It would help him in the business, but he was stuck on the financing. His ex-wife had run up a large number of bills on a joint credit card and the credit card company was coming after him for her shopping sprees. In order to finance the car he needed to have a co-signer involved, due to his suddenly poor credit score. Lars wondered whom Donna might suggest.

Ever the friend, Donna indicated that she could co-sign. She did the books and knew how much Lars was earning. There could never be a problem with him making a $300-per-month car payment.

Lars insisted that he was not asking Donna to sign, he was merely inquiring as to whom she thought he should ask to co-sign. Donna then insisted that Lars look no further. She thought she should co-sign. She was willing to help Lars because she trusted him and she prided herself for helping her friends in need.

Lars was very appreciative. The next day after work they went to the dealership and signed the papers for the new Dodge Durango. As Donna was sitting down to sign, the credit manager asked her if she understood the consequences of what she was signing. He explained that if Lars didn't make the payments for any reason Donna would become responsible for them. Donna acknowledged this as she co-signed for the Durango. She knew Lars's character and income. There wouldn't be a problem.

Lars drove the SUV off the lot. Donna followed in her car. They went to the nicest restaurant in town to celebrate. When Lars tried to pay for the meal on his credit card, it was rejected. He grumbled again at his ex-wife's profligate ways as Donna paid for dinner.

In the next few weeks Lars seemed to drift away from Donna. He wasn't as attentive or flirtatious. She thought it was due to the increased pressures of the job. With the new Durango, he was probably making a better impression and thus was even busier. Donna didn't worry about it too much, although she did miss the attention.

Then, one Monday, Lars failed to come to work. Everyone thought he was sick. One of the painters joked that he probably had the "bourbon flu," since he had seen Lars drinking heavily on Saturday night.

Tuesday, Wednesday . . . still no Lars. No calls to him were answered, so on Thursday one of the owners went over to Lars's apartment. The manager said he had cleared out late Saturday night without notice. Monies were owed, and if Lars was found the building manager wanted notice of his whereabouts. On Friday, Donna got a call from the auto finance company. Lars had missed his first payment on the Durango. They wanted her to cover it the next day.

Donna was shocked and dismayed. She had tried to help a friend. How could this happen? She made the first payment, hoping that Lars would turn up or call, or somehow take responsibility for the remaining payments.

Two months and two payments later, Donna got her answer. The Durango was found, totaled, in a ditch, a thousand miles away. Lars was in jail for driving under the influence. He claimed he didn't remember a thing.

Lars had also let his insurance lapse. He had no money. Pursuant to the co-signed agreement, the auto finance company sought payment for the entire vehicle and other costs from Donna. They demanded tens of thousands of dollars from her immediately.

Donna had to go deep into debt to pay off the Durango. In all, she lost her nest egg and savings for her long-awaited home purchase. Her credit score was so negatively affected she had to put off buying a home for what seemed like an eternity.

All for helping a friend.

When someone asks you to co-sign for them, think about yourself first. Think about what it would do to your credit if the full amount owed were suddenly due. After all, you've got a credit score to protect.

Credit Scores

While your credit report is important, the numbers that are created from your credit report—your credit scores—are even more important. Credit scores are mysterious and often misunderstood. But they're so important that it's worth taking the time to understand them.

How Much Is a Good Credit Score Worth?

Here's an example of how much money a good credit score can save you on a $150,000, thirty-year home loan:

FICO score	APR	Monthly Payment	Total Interest Paid
720–850	6.238	$922	$182,066
700–719	6.363	$935	$186,466
675–699	6.900	$988	$205,644
620–674	8.050	$1106	$248,117
560–619	8.531	$1157	$266,400
500–559	9.289	$1238	$295,772

Example based on data as of May 18, 2004. *Permission to reprint information granted by Informa Research Services, Inc., 26565 Agoura Road #300, Calabasas, CA 91302, www.informars.com. The information has been obtained from various financial institutions and Informa Research Services cannot guarantee the accuracy of such information.*

Look at the difference between the interest you'll pay if you are in the top score category versus what you'll pay if you are at the bottom—over $110,000! It pays to have a strong credit score.

Most people by now have heard of FICO scores. They're the scores created by the Fair Isaac Company (hence the acronym). FICO scores have been around for many years and they're the most widely used general type of scores. But you don't have a single FICO score because different FICO-based scores can be created depending on who is using them, and for what purpose.

There's one goal in creating a score, and that's to predict behavior. In most cases, lenders, employers, or insurance companies are using scores to predict the risk in lending money (or extending insurance, or giving a job) to a consumer. But they can also use scores to predict how profitable a current or prospective customer might be, to predict what will happen if you increase a customer's credit line or change the terms of an account, and so on.

Scores are created by analyzing the factors that different groups of consumers have in common. The goal is to find which factors those who pay their bills on time have in common, as well as the factors those who *don't* pay on time, share. Often FICO scores are based on information in the credit report, but they can also include information in an application or in customers' account histories.

On the plus side, there is simply no way credit would be as easily available as it is today if credit reports and scores didn't exist. If you need to borrow for emergencies—or for good debt—credit scoring makes it possible to get a loan quickly. Credit scoring is objective, and for the most part, unbiased. There are concerns that it is skewed against recent immigrants or minorities who may not have established a traditional credit file. But that may be changing with the creation of a new credit bureau, PRBC, as we explain in the next chapter.

Here are some basics to know about credit scoring:

- **It all depends.** Most of us think of credit scores as a "scorecard"—in other words, like a golf game where you tally up your strokes and see what your score is. But it's not so simple. In fact, there is a tremendous amount of data-crunching that goes into creating these systems. The most important thing to understand is that *every factor is interdependent on the other data that's available.* It's like a golf game where each stroke was based not only on the fact that you swing at the ball but also on wind factors, lighting, and gallery noise.

We tend to think of credit scores in direct terms . . . if I do X, then my score will improve (or go up by) x number of points. With a score, though, the effect of an action like closing an account or paying off an account will depend on the other items in the file.

Here's an example. You may have heard that each inquiry on your file drops your score by 3 or 5 points, or some other number. That may happen. But it might not. How much your score will drop—if at all—based on a new credit inquiry depends on the type of inquiry as well as all the other factors in the credit report.

- **Logic doesn't apply.** While we often try to understand credit scores in logical terms such as "too many credit inquiries makes it look as though you're shopping for too much credit," the truth is it all comes down to numbers. Information in the score is evaluated to predict risk. If it helps do that, it will be included in the score. If not, it won't.

Here's an example of this. FICO determined a few years ago that the fact that a person has been through credit counseling is not helpful in predicting future risk. So they no longer include it when calculating a score.

I am not saying that credit scores are completely illogical, though it can seem that way. It just means that arguing with the explanations of why something is included (or not) is not helpful.

If you are turned down for credit or insurance (or charged more) based on a score, by law you are supposed to be given the top four reasons that contributed to your score. But even those can be confusing. If the reason is "too many retail accounts," for example, that leads to the question "how many are too many?" There's no specific number that FICO can give you, however, since it all depends on the information in your file.

But put yourself in the shoes of the Fair Isaac Company, the developers of FICO. Do you want logic to apply? The more logic used—i.e., the more definite standards there are—the more risk there is that they'll be sued. Imagine the Fair Isaac executives and their lawyers sitting in a boardroom agreeing that the more fuzzy it all is, the less the likelihood of litigation. And, in all likelihood, you'd do the same thing if you owned the company.

• **You don't have one credit score.** In fact, you have many different scores, depending on who compiled them, and when. If you've ever applied for a mortgage, for example, the lender likely ordered your credit report and score from a specialized credit bureau that could merge information from all three major credit bureaus.

In doing so, they probably received a FICO-based score from each of them. These scores were very likely all different—in some cases, quite a bit different. That's because the formulas are not exactly the same, nor is the information that goes into it. After all, a score can only be based on the information available. And since all three credit bureaus will likely have somewhat different information, as I'll explain in the next chapter, your score will be different with all three.

In the mortgage example, the lender probably took a look at the "middle" score of the three to help determine which program and/or rate you qualified for. In other cases, lenders may prefer to use a score from one particular credit reporting agency, or they may use different agencies for customers in different parts of the country.

• **Your score changes.** Every month new information is being reported to the credit bureaus and your credit report changes. It may change a lot, or a little. If you file for bankruptcy, or if one of your accounts is turned over to a collection agency, your score can drop a lot.

But it can also drop after what you think are positive changes, such as a bankruptcy or judgment falling off the report. This makes predicting what will happen if you make certain changes to your credit tough.

For example, John had a bankruptcy and two tax liens drop off his credit report after seven years. He thought his score would shoot up but it went down instead! The likely reason was that before he was in a "had a bankruptcy" group. Now he was just a consumer without much in the way of credit references.

• **More may be better.** If you've been through credit problems, you may think that avoiding credit is a good way to stay out of trouble and build better credit. But credit scoring systems must rely on the data in your report to predict how you'll handle credit in the future. If there's nothing recent to analyze, your score will suffer. Also, if you have nothing at all it is even harder to have a good credit score.

It is difficult in today's society to maintain excellent credit without a credit history. You can choose to be a recluse in the mountains, but that is an option for very few. The rest of us have to be concerned about our credit profiles and our credit scores.

Currently you are better off having a number of credit successes. Generally speaking, four or five different types of accounts paid on time over time will make for a stronger score than if you only have one. Include a major credit card in that mix, and perhaps a car loan, mortgage, retail card, and another type of loan.

This doesn't mean you should open a bunch of accounts at once. Doing so can also have a negative effect on your credit in the short term. But if your credit history is skimpy and your score reflects that, you may want to add some positive references.

What's in a Credit Score?

With a FICO-based score, the higher the number, the better your score. Scores above 720 are usually considered excellent (850 is usually tops), those in the 680–720 range are still quite good, while those in the 650–680 range aren't terrible, but will carry higher rates. Once you start getting below

650 you may have some trouble getting credit or be charged high rates. These are general rules of thumb, though, since every lender has different criteria.

According to Fair Isaac Company, five categories of information (along with their relative weightings) go into your credit score:

Payment history	35%
Amounts you owe	30%
Length of credit history	15%
New credit	10%
Type of credit in use	10%

It's obvious that your payment history is the most important factor in your score. But there are some finer points here that you may not be aware of:

- Most lenders don't report you as late to the credit bureaus until you fall behind by 30 days. (But they will often charge you a hefty late fee if you are just one hour late with your payment!) This isn't a hard-and-fast rule so always be sure to double-check if you're having trouble meeting the due date. Sometimes lenders will close your account or up your rate if you are chronically late, even by just a few days.
- Recent late payments, even for small amounts, hurt your credit score significantly.
- Late payments will generally remain for seven years, even if you catch up on the account or pay off the bill. See the next chapter for details.
- All other things being equal, how many months you fell behind is more important than the amount. For example, missing a $20 minimum payment for 4 months in a row will probably impact your score more than missing a $300 car payment one time.

Account balances, however, play more of a role in a score than most people realize. It's not uncommon to hear "I have excellent credit" from a consumer who has paid on time but has a ton of debt—and whose score is suffering as a result. There are several factors that will come into play in this evaluation:

- How close you are to your limits on your revolving accounts such as credit cards and lines of credit. The closer you are to your limits, the worse it can be for the score.

- How much you owe on your total revolving lines of credit. Total up all your available revolving lines of credit and then total your outstanding balances. As you use 50 percent or more of your available credit on your revolving accounts, your score can start to suffer.

- How much you owe compared to other consumers across the country.

When you review your credit report, you'll see some creditors won't report a credit limit, or they will report it as zero. This is for competitive reasons (they don't want other issuers knowing your credit limits), but it can create problems in calculating an accurate debt-to-available-credit ratio. If you find this on your credit report, I recommend you complain to the credit grantor and to the FTC at www.ftc.gov.

☞ *Credit Maximizer Tip:* You don't have to carry debt to build credit! You do need credit cards as credit references, but you don't have to carry balances on them. You can use the cards you have for things you'd normally buy, pay them off in full, and avoid bad debt.

The obvious advice is to try to keep your balances, especially on your revolving debt like credit cards (which is often bad debt anyway), down. But there's also another piece of advice that goes along with this: Be cautious about closing old accounts.

Closing Accounts

If you've had credit for a while, you'll almost always find old accounts you don't use anymore listed as still open on your credit report. Unless you actually tell the lender you want to close your credit cards, they probably won't. (They'd love it if you'd use them again!) But if you do ask, they have to list them as closed at your request.

But is this best for your credit? Maybe not. Fair Isaac Company has said that closing old accounts can never help your credit score and can only hurt it. If you talk with a savvy mortgage broker, however, you'll hear how they had a client who closed some inactive accounts and boosted her credit score. But it can hurt your credit score, for three reasons:

- You'll probably close the older accounts. While closing an account does *not* remove it from your credit history, once closed, those old accounts may drop off your credit history and this will shorten the average length of your credit history. With credit scores, a longer report is better.
- I've already explained that credit scores look at your available credit to outstanding debt ratio. Close some accounts and you may appear closer to your total available credit limits. FICO scores don't care about how much total credit you have available, though individual lenders may take that into account.
- Closing accounts may leave you with too few credit references.

Here's an actual e-mail from a mortgage broker about his client's experiences with closing accounts:

"I had an interesting day. First thing this morning I ran a credit report for one of my customers and got scores of 648, 677, and 684. She couldn't understand why her credit scores were so low since she ran her credit just two months ago and got all scores in the 700–710 range. Since I couldn't see any reason at all why her score had gone down, no late payments and not a lot of other credit available, I asked her if she had closed any credit cards lately. It turned out that she had just closed what was most likely her oldest card. I don't see any other reason her credit took such a drop so this must have been the cause.

"I was telling this story to a colleague and she had a very different story. A couple months ago she ran her report and got scores around 570. She had seventeen open credit cards and a lot of available credit but not one late payment. She closed seven credit cards and was smart (or lucky) enough to close the new ones and keep the old ones. This month her credit score went up to 640.

"My guess is that in both cases the change in credit was so large because they are both very young and don't have a lot of credit history. I doubt that there would be so much of a change in either case if they had twenty to thirty years of credit but who knows?"

If you really want to close out those inactive accounts, do it one by one—perhaps no more than one every six months. FICO recommends you start by closing retail cards rather than major credit cards, and close more recent ones rather than older ones. Leave several open for emergencies as well as for a better credit history.

Inquiries

Whenever a company requests your credit report, an inquiry is created. There are two main types of inquiries: hard inquiries (which companies that request your credit report will see) and soft inquiries (which no one but you sees). Hard inquiries *will* affect your credit score while soft inquiries *won't*.

SOFT INQUIRIES
Soft inquiries include:

- Promotional inquiries: When your file is used for a prescreened (pre-approved) credit offer.
- Account review: When your lenders review your file.
- Consumer-initiated: When you order your own report.

Inquiries from employers and insurance companies may be hard inquiries, but don't count in your credit score.

MORTGAGE AND AUTO-RELATED INQUIRIES
Shopping on the Internet for a mortgage or car loan can create lots of inquiries, something you need to be careful of. Also, when you go car shopping, it's not uncommon for the dealer to access your credit file. Sometimes they even do that without your permission or knowledge, so watch out!

Fair Isaac Company has created a program to address this. All mortgage- and auto-related inquiries within the most recent thirty-day period are ignored, while mortgage-related inquiries or auto-related inquiries within a fourteen-day period (before the most recent thirty-day period) are treated as a single inquiry. There is no special protection when it comes to shopping for credit cards or other types of loans.

Note: If mortgage- or auto-related inquiries can't be identified as such, this buffer won't help. Also, if the lender is using older credit scoring software that doesn't incorporate these changes, it won't help.

Getting Your Credit Score

If you want to get your credit score, you'll generally have to pay for it. The charge should be minimal. If you're thinking about buying a house or car, it would be a good idea to get a credit score from all three bureaus (see next chapter).

NextGen Scores

Fair Isaac has created newer credit scoring models called NextGen. They have been available to creditors for a while, but are not widely used yet. They say that these NextGen scores are even better at predicting behavior, and that most consumers have a higher score under the NextGen scoring models than they do under the FICO models. Currently, though, there is no way to take a look at your NextGen-based score or know which creditors are using that system. That will change as they become more commonplace.

Insurance Bureau Scores

Some 95 percent of auto insurers, and many homeowner's insurance companies, use insurance bureau scores to help decide if you'll get insurance, as well as the rate you'll pay. There is a lot of controversy around this issue. Some elderly drivers, for example, who had never filed claims have been dropped by their auto insurers due to their low insurance bureau scores. It's not that they had bad credit, they just never used credit much at all, so their scores were low.

Here is an example of what can happen: Agnes and her husband, Bill, always worked hard and saved their money. When they retired, they decided to travel, purchased a new vehicle, and started seeing the country. For the first time, they obtained a credit card just for emergencies on the road. Their daughter watched their home and checked their mail while they were gone. They called her faithfully every Sunday from the road. One week their daughter reported she had bad news. Their insurance company had decided not to renew their insurance policy on the truck. Their daughter had already called the family's insurance agent and learned that even though their driving record was spotless, the insurance company was now relying on credit scores to rate drivers. Even though Agnes and Bill had excellent credit, they were being dropped for lack of credit experience! The agent was going to find another policy but warned their daughter that credit scores were commonly used these days.

In addition, there's always the issue of accuracy. If your credit report is inaccurate or you're a victim of fraud, that information will influence your score. You may be paying more for insurance and not know why.

Usually a credit score and insurance bureau score will fall into similar categories. In other words, if you have a good credit score, you should have a good insurance bureau score—but not always.

If you are denied insurance, or your rate is raised as a result of an insurance score, you *must* be told that and given information on how to contact the credit bureau that supplied your file. Insist on that—it's your right.

If you don't like the idea of your bill-paying history being used to determine your insurance rates, visit www.insurancescored.com, a consumer advocacy Web site. This site will inform you as to current efforts to curb such practices. Beyond that, the only thing you can do is to take our advice and start building better credit. Better credit usually means a better insurance bureau score.

Warning: Some consumers have been taken by the "false credit score scam." A car dealership checks their credit. They are then told that their score is lower than it really is and given more expensive financing. Another alternative is for the dealership to use its own custom version of a FICO-based score, which turns out to be lower than the score with the bureaus. Your best self-defense? Always check your own credit scores *before* you shop for a loan, and apply for pre-approved financing with a lender before you start looking for a car. Be prepared for the fact that some unethical individuals misuse credit information and you have to watch out for yourself.

Chapter X

Credit Reports: Your Lifelong Report Card

Whether you're a real estate investor, business owner, or just a consumer who has paid bills, you have a credit report. And that report is probably more important to your financial life than any report card you ever received in school. In fact, it plays a key role in what kind of credit you get and how much you pay. Even if you don't ever borrow or use a credit card, it likely affects how much you pay for your auto and homeowner's insurance. So you have to know what's in your credit report, as well as how credit reports work.

Credit reporting agencies (also commonly called credit bureaus) are in the business of compiling information about people's bill-paying habits and selling that information to other companies that may want to extend credit, insurance, or even a job offer to them.

There are three major national credit reporting agencies in the United States: Equifax, Experian (formerly TRW), and TransUnion. Plus there are hundreds of smaller credit bureaus that are affiliated with one or more of these "Big Three." These specialized agencies get information from one or more of the three major bureaus and may supply additional credit information as well. (See the end of this chapter for more information on other consumer reporting agencies.)

There are also business credit bureaus; Dun & Bradstreet and Experian are the main two that compile reports solely on businesses around the world. To learn more about business credit reports, see the Resources section for helpful Web sites. Our focus here is on personal credit, though it can be extremely valuable to build business credit as well.

Credit reporting is big business, and the major credit reporting agencies are businesses in competition with one another. They are all trying to make their reports better than the others and they will not share information unless they are required to do so by law. That's one reason why, when you check your credit report, you'll see that it looks somewhat different depending on which bureau supplied it. While most of the agencies will likely show similar information, their reports won't all be exactly the same.

Credit reporting agencies are regulated under the federal Fair Credit Reporting Act (FCRA), which was updated in 1999 and again at the end of December 2003 under the Fair and Accurate Credit Transactions Act. You'll learn more about your rights under that law in this chapter and the next.

Starting Out

Margery and Sharon were college roommates. They attended a large, Midwestern university—but that was where the similarities ended. Margery was prudent, studious, and focused. Sharon was a party girl, living for the moment and enjoying every one of them.

While Margery thought nothing of studying on a Saturday night if her courses so required, Sharon was out all Saturday night and into Sunday morning. There was friction when Sharon brought friends over to their small house off-campus to finish off the night. Margery needed her sleep and let Sharon know about it.

Not surprisingly, Margery and Sharon were also different in their spending habits. Margery had saved to attend college and was fortunate enough to get a partial scholarship to help defray the costs. She did not want to burden her parents and was proud that she had not asked them for money. Margery did not want to incur a great deal of debt and avoided obtaining a credit card, being instead cautious and prudent in her spending.

Sharon, on the other hand, was anything but prudent. She lived off student loans, her parents' money, and in the last year, three high-interest credit cards. Since they were recently maxed out, she told Margery that she would have to get another one to help with next month's rent. Margery asked how she could handle all the high-interest payments. Sharon explained that working at the Rat, the local rathskeller and college hangout, on the prime party nights of Thursday and Friday provided enough tip money to make the monthly payments. The principal payments, like her student loans, she'd worry about later.

Margery privately worried that Sharon was headed for trouble. She was again thankful of her resolve to avoid credit cards and credit problems.

Soon graduation arrived and both of them found decent starting jobs in Chicago. They agreed not to be roommates, both acknowledging that their lifestyles were a bit too different, but did agree to keep in touch.

Margery soon ran into difficulty finding an apartment. When the management companies did a check of her credit, she didn't turn up. While there wasn't any negative information, there also wasn't any positive information either on which to base a decision. She had no credit history, which, as Margery soon learned, was a negative.

Sharon called and invited Margery over to, of course, a party at her new apartment. Margery was pleased to be included with her old group of friends and, even more so, was curious about how Sharon, with her negative credit, had found an apartment so quickly. Arriving, she found that Sharon had moved into a spacious one-bedroom apartment with a large balcony and an excellent view. Greeting Sharon, Margery couldn't help but ask how she lined up such a great apartment. Sharon replied that the manager said she had great credit because she made all of her credit card payments on time.

Margery woke up the next morning realizing she had to get a credit card. If four cards worked for Sharon, at least one card would work for her. She called a bank to begin the process. The bank checked her credit and politely declined her. Margery was getting frustrated and wanted to know why she was declined, especially since she had been sent hundreds of credit card solicitations during college. The representative explained that college students were of a different credit class. She was out of college, with no prior credit history, and thus, according to their standards, not entitled to a credit card.

Margery was at her wit's end. Was there anything she could do? She asked the representative. Yes, came the reply. A credit card, secured by a $2,500 deposit, could be obtained. It worked just like a credit card, the representative brightly noted.

Margery was close to tears. She needed all her extra cash for a security deposit on an apartment. She couldn't waste it on a credit card, no matter how much she needed to build credit. Margery hung up and, swallowing her pride, called home.

Margery's father flew to Chicago the next weekend. Together they found a nice, affordable apartment, which he—with his established credit—co-signed. Calling around, they found a secured credit card with only a $500 deposit requirement. If a good payment history was established over a one-year period, the deposit would be returned and credit would be granted. Margery's father encouraged her to charge her groceries on the card and pay the resulting monthly bill promptly, thus establishing a payment history for some computer somewhere to latch on to.

Margery thanked her father and promised not to burden him. He said he was genuinely pleased that she called for his help.

Margery set about getting her apartment ready. When she called the power company to establish an account, they did a credit check. Now a credit warrior, Margery knew the response before it was given. Sure enough, due to a lack of credit history, a $300 deposit was required.

Margery now had to laugh at the absurdity of it all. She called Sharon to tell her about the new apartment. Amid the conversation, Margery asked if Sharon had to pay a deposit to the power company. No, replied Sharon, a deposit was waived for good credit.

You first build a credit report when you fill out a credit application and the company orders a credit report on you. If there is no information in their databases, they will store your basic identifying information—name, address, and Social Security number. Once you do get a loan that is reported, that information will then be sent to one or more of the major reporting agencies to start your credit file.

For a fast way to establish credit, see the "Building Credit" section in the next chapter.

How to Get Your Credit Report

The Fair and Accurate Credit Transactions Act of 2003 (which updates the federal Fair Credit Reporting Act), requires every major national credit bureau to give each consumer a free credit report per year. In addition, you can order a free copy of your report from bureaus that compile reports on:

- Medical records or payments
- Residential or tenant history
- Check writing history (such as ChexSystems or TeleCheck)—discussed later in this chapter
- Employment history
- Insurance claims (such as C.L.U.E.—see discussion later in this chapter).

At the time of this writing, free reports were expected to be rolled out in different parts of the country, starting in late 2004 through late 2005. For updated information on how to order your free report, check www.success dna.com. In addition, you can get a free copy of your report when:

- You have been denied credit or other benefits, or have received notice of a change of your credit status, in the last sixty days.
- You are unemployed, receiving welfare, or have been denied employment.
- You believe you are a victim of fraud (fraud victims get two free reports a year).
- You are notified that you did not qualify for the lender's best rate or terms based on information in your credit report.

You can get information about ordering your credit report directly from any of the three major credit bureaus at:

- www.equifax.com
- www.experian.com
- www.transunion.com

☞ *Credit Maximizer Tip:* If you are going to buy a home or car, invest in real estate, or make another major purchase, get your credit report immediately. It can sometimes take sixty days to clear up mistakes. If you are a real estate investor, it can pay to subscribe to a service that monitors your credit report each month. Visit SuccessDNA.com for a referral.

Who Gets Your Report?

With all the sensitive information in credit reports, you'd think companies would need your permission, maybe even written permission, to get your credit report. Not so.

The Fair Credit Reporting Act allows companies to obtain a credit report for:

- Employment purposes (by a prospective or current employer). Here they do need your written permission first.
- Insurance underwriting purposes (including when your policy is up for renewal).
- Considering your application for credit, or to review or collect an existing credit account (this could include applying for cell phone service, for example).
- A legitimate business purpose in connection with a business transaction initiated by the consumer.
- Per court order or in conjunction with certain requests involving child support.

While there are lots of sources for ordering your own credit report, it's harder to get credit reports on other people. If you want to purchase consumer credit reports, for example, on prospective renters for your properties, you can go through a local agency that supplies credit reports for that purpose. It is illegal to get a report on, say, your fiancé or your ex without their permission, but it might not be terribly difficult to do either. (Don't do it, though. The penalties can be severe. I just want to point out that the system isn't fail-safe.)

What's in Your Report?

There are four kinds of information in your credit report: personal information, account information, public record information, and inquiries.

PERSONAL INFORMATION
Personal information includes your:

- Full name, including Jr., Sr., or I, II, III
- Address used when requesting your credit report
- Previous addresses
- Social Security number
- Year or date of birth
- Current and former employer information
- Variations of your personal information on file, such as nicknames or former names, different Social Security numbers, different addresses, and so on.

☞ *Credit Maximizer Tip:* While it helps to make sure all your information here is correct, some information carries more weight than other information. Credit reporting agencies aren't known for keeping accurate employment records, for example, so don't sweat it too much if that's not up to date. (Although correcting it wouldn't be a bad idea either.) On the other hand, if there's a Social Security number that doesn't belong to you, you'll want to get that taken off as quickly as possible since it could indicate fraud.

ACCOUNT INFORMATION
Account information is a list of accounts (called "tradelines" in the industry) you currently have or have had in the past, including:

- Account name and number
- Date opened, closed
- Monthly payment amount rounded off to the nearest dollar
- Monthly payment history, usually covering at least twenty-four months
- Current status of account (paid as agreed, thirty days late, and so on)

The types of accounts that normally appear on your credit report are:

- Credit cards, retail or department store cards, gas company cards
- Bank loans
- Auto loans and leases
- Mortgages and home equity loans or lines
- Consumer finance company accounts
- Recreational vehicle loans
- Credit union credit cards or loans
- Student loans

Types of accounts that do not generally appear on your standard credit report:

- Rent-to-own accounts
- Checking account information
- Accounts with smaller institutions
- Rental payment history
- Utilities or cell phone accounts, unless sent to collection
- Medical bills, unless delinquent
- Child support, unless delinquent

Important: No law requires that lenders report to credit reporting agencies. Some report to only one or two bureaus, while others only report if you fall behind. There are also specialized bureaus for checking account information, which we'll describe later.

PUBLIC RECORD INFORMATION
Public record and collections information may include:

- Court judgments
- Federal, state, and county liens, including tax liens
- Bankruptcy filings
- Collection accounts

Public record information is a little different from account information in that there is no account number, credit limit, or payment history. There's no rating, either, but these listings are considered negative.

There can be a lot of room for error here. One woman, for example, moved from California to Florida. A few years later she discovered that the state of California determined she owed an extra $100 on her state income tax. But since they didn't have her current address, they had gone ahead and got a judgment against her. (By this time it was over $400 including penalties). She paid it off, but two years later the judgment had never been listed as satisfied on her credit report and created additional problems because it looked like she still owed it.

Collection accounts are another problem. Frequently, they are not listed when paid when they have been, or they are not listed as being in dispute when the consumer has legitimately disputed them.

By the way, employers can review your credit report if they get your written permission first. They cannot, however, turn you down for a job just because you filed for bankruptcy (though some apparently don't know the law because they do!).

INQUIRIES

Inquiries list the companies that have seen your credit report in the past two years. It's not unusual to see companies you don't recognize in this section. First of all, companies don't need your written permission to access your credit file. They just need a legitimate credit, insurance, or employment purpose. Requesting a new cell phone account could create an inquiry on your file, for example.

Also, the company actually accessing your report may have a different name. For example, you go into your local Dave's Flooring and apply for an account to buy new carpet for your home. That financing may be handled by XYZ Finance Co., which is what's listed on your credit report. As we discussed in the last chapter, only hard inquiries, or inquiries where you actually apply for credit, hurt your credit score.

☞ *Credit Maximizer Tip:* Inquiries from companies you don't recognize could be an early sign of credit fraud so don't hesitate to ask the credit reporting agency for more information and contact that company, if necessary, to find out why it reviewed your file.

Ratings Codes

When you get your report, most of the information will likely be spelled out in plain English. But the codes that have been around for years are still sometimes used so it's helpful to know what they are.

Open account (usually must be paid in full in 30, 60, or 90 days)	0
Revolving account	R
Installment account	I
Mortgage	M
Line of credit	C

Numeric codes for current payment status:

Payment Status	Code
Not rated, too new to rate, or not used	00
Paid as agreed	01
Paid 30 days late, or not more than one payment past due	02
Paid 60 days late, or two payments past due	03
Paid 90 days late, or three payments past due	04
Paid 120 days late	05
Making regular payments under a wage earner bankruptcy plan or credit counseling plan	07
Repossession	08
Voluntary repossession	8A
Legal repossession	8D

Payment to a repossessed account	8P
Repossession redeemed	8R
Bad debt; charged-off account	09
Collection account	9B
Payment to a charged-off account	9P
Unrated	UR
Unclassified	UC
Rejected	RJ

Clearly, you want as many R1s and I1s on your report as possible! They show your credit history is current.

Your payment history is the most important section of your report, so you want to look at it carefully to make sure it's accurate. The sooner you spot mistakes, the more time you'll have to straighten them out (and it does take time). We'll explain how to do that in a later chapter.

How Long Can Information Be Reported?

If you have damaged credit, this is probably really important to you: How long can that bad information stay on your report?

THE LONG SHADOW OF CREDIT

Roberto had made some mistakes. He had taken some risks on a restaurant that didn't work out. The first twelve months after the business went under were tough. Roberto had been a sole proprietor and was personally responsible for every claim, whether he personally guaranteed them or not. Creditors hounded him night and day.

Roberto's attorney had told him to incorporate to limit his liability. He thought his attorney just wanted to make an extra thousand dollars off of him. Now Roberto realized that spending the thousand dollars would have saved him tens of thousands of dollars in grief and lost sleep.

The restaurant supply company sued Roberto and won a judgment of $50,000. Because they alleged fraud and prevailed, Roberto couldn't dismiss the claim in bankruptcy. He paid $1,000 a month for five years to satisfy the judgment. His quality of life suffered greatly for those five years.

The other vendors—the produce company, the linen company, the landlord, and the like, all threatened to sue. For six months Roberto had dealt with angry business owners. He had held them off by telling them the truth—he didn't have any money. Roberto was wiped out.

Then attack-dog collection agencies stepped in. The vendors had turned their claims over to some not very pleasant people who sneered hatred over the phone. These people, in violation of the law, called Roberto late at night and threatened all forms of damnation if he didn't pay off the debts.

For another six months Roberto had weathered these calls. He told the truth. He didn't have any money. The collection agencies threatened to sue. Roberto said that was their right. The collection agencies threatened to ruin Roberto's credit rating. Roberto said that it was already ruined.

Eventually Roberto developed a twisted philosophical—and useful—sense of the collection game. The collection agencies were paid to be nasty people, doing a nasty-paying job. They had issues. While Roberto had failed once, he was still a moral person and thus superior in spirit to the venomous voices on the other side. He developed a calm in dealing with the collection agencies. The more they yelled and demanded, the more peaceful Roberto's responses became. The calmer he became, the more truly angry some of the collection agents got. Their bile and invective and voice levels became scary, even psychotic. But Roberto remained calm. He had learned that those whom the gods would destroy they first make angry. By the end of some calls Roberto worried that the collector would go straight home and kick the dog. But that wasn't his problem.

After a year, the calls from business owners and their collection agencies tapered off. Some had followed through on their threats to place a nonpayment on his credit report. The report now read like an F in Money 101.

The last seven years had not been easy. Roberto had gone back to being a pastry chef. He worked hard for five years to pay off the $50,000 lawsuit. His credit was so poor he couldn't begin to buy a house or a car, so he lived in a modest apartment and took the bus to work.

During the last two years, with the lawsuit now paid off, Roberto's financial situation had improved. He was saving money to buy a car with cash. How he would pay for auto insurance he wasn't sure of, beyond providence taking care of him.

Then Roberto got another call. He knew from the sneering tone that it was from a bill collector. The voice demanded the linen company be paid $10,000 immediately or litigation would ensue. The voice claimed that the linen company would easily prevail in court, and, with interest penalties and attorney's fees, a total of $20,000 would be owed. Roberto remained calm. He asked a logical question. How long are these debts due? The collector became very angry. He shouted that the debts were due forever from deadbeats and that his credit report would show it into eternity. He told Roberto that he had twenty-four hours to decide between $10,000 or $20,000 and slammed down the phone.

Roberto had a sense that something wasn't quite right. He hadn't learned it in school—unfortunately school had taught him nothing about money—but it seemed that at some point a debt obligation ended. It seemed to Roberto that after a certain number of years he should be free of such claims.

Roberto decided to see his attorney for advice. He'd rather spend $200 than $10,000, if possible.

The attorney informed Roberto that there was a set period of time after which debt obligations expired, in legal jargon, the statute of limitations, or a time period by which something had to occur. While each state had a different time period for various matters, in Roberto's state the statute of limitations for collecting on the type of debt in question was seven years.

Roberto said that seven years had already passed. The attorney acknowledged that point and commented that the other time period of note was the seven and one half years for credit reports. Roberto wondered aloud how credit reports fit into it. The collection agent had said the debt would be reported forever.

The attorney laughed. He had dealt with liars for twenty years and no class of liar was more brazen than bill collectors who misrepresented that debts stayed on your credit report forever. The attorney informed Roberto that the debt fell off a credit report after seven and one half years.

Roberto was now angry. The collection agent was trying to trick him into paying a debt that was outside the statute of limitations, thus legally not owed, and was soon to be off his credit report. The lawyer nodded and commented that it happened all the time. Collection agencies would search the records for debts that were seven years old and try to collect them through trickery. In fact, it was such a problem that the Federal Trade Commission encouraged Americans to report such abuses at www.ftc.gov.

Roberto was only too happy to do so. And, in another four months, his credit report was cleared of his restaurant venture. Roberto felt free once again, and looked forward to buying his first home.

Credit reports can cast a long shadow, so it is important to know how long information remains in your file. Here's what the federal Fair Credit Reporting Act says:

• Bankruptcy: All personal bankruptcies can remain ten years from the filing date (not the discharge date, which is when the bankruptcy ends). If you filed Chapter 13, however, and paid back some of your debts over a few years, then you can ask the credit reporting agencies to remove your bankruptcy seven years from the date of filing. Most will if asked.

• Civil suits or civil judgments: Seven years from the date of entry (by the court), or the current governing statute of limitations, whichever is longer. Often credit bureaus will remove these seven years from the date of entry if they are paid.

• Paid tax liens: Seven years from the date satisfied (or released).

• Unpaid tax liens: Indefinitely until the lien is paid, then the seven years above kicks in.

• Collection or charge-off accounts: No longer than seven years.

• Late payments: No longer than seven years.

• Delinquent student loans: If you bring a defaulted federally insured student loan current and make twelve consecutive on-time payments, and are not late for *any* reason, you can then have the previous late payments wiped out.

• Positive or neutral information: May be reported indefinitely.

SEVEN YEARS FROM WHEN?

This gets confusing. One consumer received an e-mail from one of the largest credit reporting agencies saying that collection accounts would be reported for seven years from the date of last activity. But what does date of last activity mean? The last time a payment was made? The last time she used the account? The FCRA doesn't mention date of last activity, but you may hear it from time to time. Attorneys at the Federal Trade Commission have commented that date of last activity does not determine how long information can remain on your report. If a credit bureau tells you otherwise, report that to the FTC at www.ftc.gov. Be as specific in your complaint as you can be.

The FCRA spells out very specific rules for how long collection or charged-off accounts can be reported: *7 years and 180 days (roughly six months) from the date the payment was due leading up to the charge-off or collection account.* Note that it does *not* start when the account was placed for collection or from the date of last activity.

Example: Let's say you first fell behind on your January 2000 payment on your SkyHigh Bank credit card. You didn't make your payments so in June 2000, the bank charged off your account. In December 2000 it was sent to ToughTimes Collection Agency. That delinquency and collection account can remain on your report for seven and a half years from January 2000—the date the payment was due.

Collection agencies are required by law to report the original date of delinquency. If you can't tell what it is from your report, ask the credit bureau. If it's not there, dispute it! That's the only way they can tell how long to report those accounts.

Also, don't let collection agencies tell you they can report information forever. Those accounts fall off after seven and a half years whether you pay them or not. If a collection agency tells you otherwise, report them to the Federal Trade Commission at www.ftc.gov.

Other Consumer Reporting Agencies

INNOVIS

Innovis Data Solutions, when it's mentioned, is often referred to as a fourth credit bureau. It's not well known, and in fact it's hard to find information about Innovis and what it does. Currently it does not provide credit reports directly to lenders. Instead, it sells lists that credit card companies and other businesses can use for their marketing. For example, it sells a list of people who have moved recently, as well as a list of people who have been delinquent on their accounts (to be used as an additional screening for pre-approved credit card offers).

You're not going to be denied credit based on your Innovis report. But you could be taken off lists for the most favorable offers, so it's a good idea while you're checking your credit report to review your Innovis file as well. Instructions can be found at www.innovis.com.

PRBC: A NEW CREDIT BUREAU

Pay Rent, Build Credit, Inc. is a new credit bureau that for the first time plans to report rent payments and other payments such as utilities, phone, auto loans, mobile home loans, and day care. You can sign up for free at their Web site (www.payrentbuildcredit.com) and build your file either by:

- Taking proof of payment to participating partners such as financial institutions or credit counselors who can verify it,
- Using a participating online banking service, or
- Renting from a participating landlord.

This new credit bureau can become a godsend for consumers who have had trouble establishing credit the traditional way. The information they collect will be used by the other credit bureaus to supplement their files, or sold to lenders considering you for credit—but only with your okay first. The PRBC system can also be used by business owners to build business credit reports.

☞ *Credit Maximizer Tip:* If you are currently renting, or have a skimpy credit report, sign up for PRBC free on their Web site, www.payrent buildcredit.com. If you are a real estate investor with lease option tenants in your home, encourage them to sign up so they can build their credit and buy your property!

CHEXSYSTEMS AND TELECHECK

If you've ever bounced a check, that information won't show up in a traditional credit report. But it may appear in a consumer report prepared by ChexSystems or TeleCheck. Some 19 million Americans have negative information in their ChexSystems report and don't know it. (TeleCheck also collects information about checking accounts, but is smaller.)

ChexSystems and TeleCheck collect information about consumers who have had problems with their checking or banking accounts (usually overdrawn accounts that have been closed by the bank). That information is often used by financial institutions to determine the risk of opening new accounts. In addition, ChexSystems also operates a company called ChexSystems Collection Agency that collects bounced checks.

You can get a free annual copy of your ChexSystems report just as you can a copy of your credit report from the three national credit bureaus.

To fix problems with your ChexSystems report, follow the same procedures as you would in disputing information on your credit report. Both ChexSystems and TeleCheck are covered by the FCRA regulations that cover credit bureaus.

If the information is accurate, and you still owe fees or charges to the financial institution that reported you, see if you can get them to agree to delete your report if you pay the balance due. Negative information will remain on file for five years and can make it difficult to open a new account elsewhere.

In addition to reviewing your ChexSystems report, some banks will also review your standard credit report when you apply to open an account. If you have had problems such as a tax lien or bankruptcy, you may want to explain it to the bank to see if that will prevent you from opening an account. Otherwise, you'll just place an unnecessary inquiry on your file.

Watch out! Even if you never bounce checks, you could end up with a negative ChexSystems report. How? If you close an account and forget about recurring fees or pre-authorized withdrawals, those charges could create an overdraft on your account that could trigger a ChexSystems report.

Bounced Out

Cheryl was in a rush that weekend. She was leaving town and needed to get to the bank in time to deposit the $600 in cash her roommate had given her for the rent. She definitely needed the money. Working as a waitress between occasional acting jobs didn't leave her with much of a cushion in the bank.

Despite her almost constant money worries, this weekend she felt flush. She was going to get away from the pressure for a carefree weekend. A friend in the travel business had invited her to stay at a posh resort with her, and the whole trip had been comped by her friend's employer. It wouldn't cost either of them a dime.

By the time Cheryl made it to the bank, the lobby and drive-through were closed. Although she had never felt comfortable depositing cash in the ATM, she needed that money in her account first thing Monday morning or a few checks were likely to bounce. So against her better judgment, she decided to go ahead and deposit it. After all, she reasoned, the bank had to have pretty strict security measures to make sure employees couldn't just walk off with her cash. As extra assurance, she held each bill up to the security camera before she put the money in the envelope and slipped it in the ATM slot.

Her weekend was perfect, without a worry. As soon as she got back in town Monday afternoon she dove back into work. The week passed by like a blur. Friday she got the mail and saw a notice from the bank. Her mind immediately began to race, wondering what it was for. As soon as she opened it, her heart fell. It was an overdraft notice.

Cheryl quickly looked up her account online to see what the problem was. The mistake was apparent immediately. Instead of a $600 cash deposit on the previous Friday, the bank listed a $100 deposit. She called the bank right away to straighten it out.

"Sorry," the manager said as Cheryl sat in his office just before closing. Her calls to the customer service number had gotten her nowhere, so she called in late for her shift at the restaurant and went directly to the branch. "We only show $100 in cash being deposited," he insisted. "But there should be a tape showing me depositing the money," Cheryl pleaded. The manager refused to budge, implying that Cheryl could have easily pocketed the difference.

Four checks Cheryl had written on the account that week had bounced. She contacted those companies to make good on the checks. In the meantime, Cheryl closed the account in anger, and refused to pay the fees the bank wanted to charge for the overdrafts. The bank, in turn, reported her information to ChexSystems.

Now, she discovered, her banking nightmare had just begun. She soon found she couldn't open an account with any local bank because of her negative credit file with ChexSystems. She began relying on friends to cash checks for her and spent hours and extra money using money orders to pay her bills. Juggling her payments became what felt like a second job. For five years, Cheryl was shut out of the normal banking world—all because someone at her bank had pocketed her cash.

GOT A CLUE?

There is a new type of credit report in our society that may totally surprise you. It is a report not on you, but rather on the property that you buy. Known as the Comprehensive Loss Underwriting Exchange, or C.L.U.E., it is an insurance industry database that insurers use to deny coverage on problem properties.

Bad Dog, Bad House

Nicolas was ready to invest in residential real estate. He had overcome some financial hurdles and in the last year had purchased his first house. It was currently his primary residence, but Nicolas purchased it with an eye to turning it into a rental when he moved to a bigger house, as he knew he would.

For now, Nicolas was looking for another single-family home to buy to generate some monthly passive income. He knew his previous financial challenges could be finally conquered with an additional $200 a month in passive income. So, Nicolas needed to find the right property at the right price.

After several weeks of diligent searching, Nicolas came across a suitable candidate. It was a three-bedroom, two-bathroom fixer-upper house, with wood floors and a large backyard that seemed to be priced $20,000 under local market comparables. And the absentee owner was willing to carry an interest-only loan for two years so the new owner could get in and fix the place.

Nicolas was interested and toured the property. He noticed a sharp, pungent odor as he entered, but after a minute or two he grew accustomed to it. The property checked out and he made an offer on it with a $2,000 down payment.

In doing his due diligence and acquisition work, Nicolas contacted his insurance broker to work on covering the property. A day later the broker called back with bad news. He couldn't cover the property due to a negative C.L.U.E. report. Since Nicolas didn't have a clue what he meant, his broker explained. In the face of record claims, the insurance industry was targeting problem properties. If a number of burglary, water or storm damage, or other claims had been filed against a property, insurers were now refusing coverage. The decision had nothing to do with the individual's credit rating, but rested solely on the property's prior claims history.

Nicolas asked what was wrong with the property. The broker explained that the owner had rented to families with dogs. Every time a family would move out the owner would submit an insurance claim for damage done by the dogs' expressions of territory. Nicolas noted the odor was pretty strong but asked why he couldn't get insurance if he agreed not to rent to dog owners anymore. The broker replied that future promises and fresh starts weren't a consideration. The property already had been marked by the insurance industry. They weren't going to go there anymore.

Nicolas appreciated the information. He backed out of the deal. Someone else would have to be clueless about the property.

It is important to note that only the current property owners can order a C.L.U.E. report (online at www.choicetrust.com). As such, buyers will want to require sellers to provide them with an insurable C.L.U.E. report. Otherwise, when you can't obtain insurance on some real estate with problems, the property's negative profile may end up sullying your own good credit. There are challenges everywhere.

Chapter XI

How to Repair Your Credit

If you're like most people, there's a good chance you'll find mistakes or problem items on your credit report. If you just have a couple of straightforward mistakes, it may be relatively easy to get them cleared up. If your problem is more complicated, or you don't have proof of your side of the story, it can take a lot longer. Some consumers have found it harder to deal with credit bureaus than with the IRS!

Carmen and Sean had excellent credit. That is until their lives were turned completely upside down.

Sean was a supervisor at the local branch of a nationally known auto parts store. Carmen was a stay-at-home mom who raised three great children, all of whom had gone to college and were now off on their own.

They were empty nesters and enjoying their time together. Then one day Carmen felt a lump in her breast. She was a little surprised but didn't act on it, thinking it may just be her imagination. Three weeks later she knew she wasn't imaging anything. Carmen's doctor confirmed it was breast cancer. An immediate mastectomy was required. They quickly obtained a second opinion from an alternative medicine clinic and just as quickly decided to stick with a traditional medicine solution. Before the couple knew what hit them they were dealing with surgery, radiation therapy, follow-up visits, and very large medical expenses.

It was at this point that Sean learned that the auto parts store had ceased providing dependent insurance coverage. Sean was shocked. Why hadn't he been notified?

The human resources assistant at the company's national headquarters said a notice had been sent out. Employees had the choice of having the cost of dependent coverage deducted from their paycheck or not. Many employees throughout the company had decided to find their own coverage for spouses and children. With over 40 percent of the employees deciding against paycheck withdrawals for dependent insurance coverage Sean's lack of a response wasn't unusual.

Sean was undone. He now had $40,000 in medical bills he thought were covered. He didn't know where to turn.

The hospital collection representative was calling Sean constantly. Carmen needed another $10,000 in treatments to battle the cancer into remission. The hospital needed to get the $50,000 paid now or they couldn't continue her life-saving treatments. Sean felt very pressured. The hospital was aggressive in their collection efforts he confided to a few friends. His friends agreed but could offer no solution to the problem. Sean was desperate. He knew he couldn't tell Carmen about the insurance coverage problem. She was recovering slowly, but was fragile. Bad news could block her progress.

Sean did what he had to do. He started scraping together as much money as possible the best he could. He liquidated the meager IRA account in a down stock market. After paying the penalties for early withdrawal of the money he had $4,000. The house had appreciated somewhat so he took out the maximum home equity line of credit he could in the amount of $20,000.

Sean still needed $26,000. The hospital collection representative was not really that pleased that he had provided them with almost half the money. Sean asked if there would be any more charges. The representative said he didn't think so. Sean asked if they would accept payments. The representative laughed and said they weren't a bank. He did suggest, however, that Sean look into a credit card that other people in his situation had used. It was a high-interest, high-fee card; it could provide him with $20,000 in credit right away.

Sean took down the name and number of the credit card company. Since the hospital collection representative was giving out advice Sean asked how he could come up with the remaining $6,000. The representative suggested that Sean avoid fully paying some regular bills for a while. Car payments, house payments could all be deferred for a time. Medical emergency was always a good excuse.

Sean knew that he had to get the money together somehow. Carmen's life depended on it.

The hospital-recommended credit card was obtained and provided another $20,000 toward the medical bills. To the remaining $6,000 he would have to completely drain his savings and then stop paying some regular bills and apply that money to paying off the hospital. Finally, in another two months the hospital was satisfied.

Sean's other creditors were not.

The mortgage company, the auto leasing company, and all his other creditors were now demanding full payment. Sean explained his predicament and how the hospital demanded money up front to finish treating his wife and how the hospital said the other creditors would understand.

The other creditors did not understand. In fact, they were angry. Medical expense emergencies were not an excuse for not paying their bills. They demanded payment.

Sean had nowhere to turn. The high-interest credit card payment and the home equity line of credit payments were both hitting him hard. He was unable to make full payment on either of them, much less his other monthly payments. He had paid the hospital to save Carmen's life, and was now losing the battle for a secure financial future.

Unable to pay creditors, his credit report scores plummeted. The report showed numerous late payments, closed accounts for failure to pay, and accounts sent to collection.

Sean's only solace was that Carmen was recovering. The price was steep, but it was worth it.

As Carmen grew stronger Sean explained their situation. She of course understood, and, as with her medical condition, she vowed to recover financially.

Carmen and Sean began to live frugally, but such a lifestyle did not compensate for the larger debts they had. Their house, burdened by both a mortgage and a home equity line of credit payment, was in the process of foreclosure. Sean had learned of a strategy whereby an investor and/or renter could clear up and take over the house payments and share in the equity when the house sold. The advantage to Sean and Carmen was that by using such a strategy their credit report would not show a foreclosure. The disadvantage to a potential partner was that with the mortgage and the line of credit there was not a great deal of equity in the house.

But Sean vowed to overcome his condition and was persistent. He found a family who had been in financial straits several years earlier. They would not be able to obtain a home loan for several more years, but they could afford the mortgage and the equity line payments. Sean worked out a deal whereby they moved into the house and took over the payments. Sean and Carmen agreed to stay on the title until the new couple could qualify for a loan. At that point, Sean and Carmen would deed the house over, allowing their obligations to be paid and allowing the new couple any benefits of appreciation on the property.

Sean and Carmen moved into much smaller quarters, a one-bedroom apartment they could afford. It wasn't what they were used to, but the kids were gone, and the house cleaning chores were much reduced. Nevertheless, they vowed it was only a temporary move. They would be back in their own house in time.

Their Buick Regal had been repossessed. That fact was a major detrimental item on his credit report. Of the twelve negative reports, the repossession of the car really stood out. Sean was a car guy and found a used car in great shape at a low price for getting around. That wasn't the problem. The problem was that if he didn't get the repossession off his report he'd never get a home loan again.

Sean decided to go right to the source. He called the credit department of the leasing company and started calmly negotiating. He questioned the amount received for the car at auction. He questioned all of the fees charged, from attorney's fees to repossession fees. (How could one repo man operating in the middle of the night ever hope to collect $175 an hour? If that was the rate, were they hiring?)

In a calm, reasoned, and likable manner he worked on the credit representative day after day. He was never angry or belligerent. He was just the opposite. He developed a rapport with the representative, who started enjoying working with a kind voice on the other end of the phone for a change.

With all the extreme and various fees a total of $10,000 was supposedly owed to the car leasing company. Sean was willing to pay 20 percent of that if they would remove the negative information from his credit report. The credit representative had to state that 20 cents on the dollar was something that they couldn't do. Sean was undeterred and kept talking. He explained the situation with his wife and the hospital, not as an excuse or for sympathy but as a matter of conversation. The credit representative was incredulous. For a hospital to withhold medical services until complete payment was made, and to represent that medical expense emergencies were a legitimate excuse to avoid the payment of other debts, was offensive. He said he would call Sean right back.

A moment later Sean had a settlement offer of 30 cents on the dollar. He accepted, relieved that a major negative was off his report.

Sean now had eleven negative statements on his credit report. He had learned that if he could get rid of at least half of them he could hope to once again qualify for a home loan. So he set about knocking them off.

The first negative report he went after was a department store payment he had missed. It was a small amount, only $189, but in the turmoil of scraping together the $50,000 for the hospital the payment had been missed and now was on his report. With interest and penalties the change had ballooned to $375. Sean spoke to the credit representative, explained his situation, and asked what they could do. The credit representative started out high but Sean got him down to $189, with an advance written promise to remove the ding from his report. Sean had learned that many creditors will say they'll re-move the item, but once paid never do. He learned it helps to have that promise in writing before paying so you can force the issue later.

The next item to resolve was a fuel company credit card. Again a payment of just $125 had been missed and it had been sent to collection. He called the collection agency representative to discuss the account, which with all the charges was now $289. The representative was rude, belligerent, and caustic. Sean had to laugh, saying that he sounded like a cliché. The representative grew even more nasty, which Sean calmly realized would happen no matter what was said. The representative was on commission and he would bully his way into payment however possible.

Sean discussed settling the account. The representative demanded full payment. Sean asked for a 30 percent discount and a written promise to re-move the negative filing from his credit report. The representative laughed bitterly and said they didn't provide any such promise until the account was paid. Sean said that was unacceptable and asked to speak to the representa-tive's supervisor. The representative shouted an obscenity and slammed down the phone.

Sean immediately called the fuel company to report the conversation. The fuel company's representative said that once the account was sent to collection it was out of their control. Sean knew that wasn't true and asked to speak to a supervisor. After waiting on hold for half of his lunch break Sean finally spoke to the supervisor. He explained that he was trying to pay off the account but that it did him no good unless he could have it removed from his credit report. He explained that the collection company's repre-sentatives used obscenities, in violation of federal law.

Sean was calm and reasonable, which the supervisor appreciated. The account was pulled back from the collection company, a firm that the super-visor admitted was a source of problems. The fuel company promised to re-move the negative credit filing upon a 70 percent payment. Sean paid the bill and another account was cleared.

Of the nine remaining negative filings four didn't really register with Sean. While things had been hectic and blurred as he was putting together enough money for Carmen's treatment, he thought he would remember all of the missed payments. But these four creditors, a stereo store, a medical clinic, a medical publisher, and an equipment leasing company, were a mystery. Sean and Carmen had looked into alternative medical treatments but they had never committed to anything. Or so they thought.

Sean sent a letter to Experian, TransUnion, and Equifax (much like the one found in Appendix B) disputing the four items he felt did not belong in his credit file. He knew that the credit reporting services and the creditors in question had thirty days to respond or the negative filing had to be removed.

As it turned out, only the stereo store responded. Sean had bought a portable CD player for Carmen and the check, like several others, had bounced. Sean took care of the payment and the negative filing was removed.

The three medical-related creditors never responded to the credit bureau's request. This did not surprise Sean. The alternative medicine clinic they had visited was a group of sleazy, fast-talking hustlers. Sean and Carmen were immediately turned off and committed to nothing. The hustlers may have tried to say they had, but no services were rendered, no ridiculous, useless "medicines" delivered.

By failing to respond to the credit bureaus' request within thirty days, the three negative (and fraudulent) reports came off.

Sean now had five negatives on his report. Two were for credit cards he had been previously late on, but were now current. The new tenant (and future owner) of his house was paying one of them regularly as part of the house deal. Sean was paying his personal credit card on a regular basis. In time the late notices would be cured by a pattern of consistent timely payments.

The remaining three negatives were not to be cured. One was to the hospital for MRI charges of $7,000, another was to a radiologist to read the MRI for $5,000, and the third was for lab work of $3,000 incurred during Carmen's follow-up visits. The $15,000 Sean vowed would never be paid. He had learned that the hospital should have never pressured him the way they did. They should have informed him that he had the right to go to another hospital for treatment instead of demanding every last nickel he had.

For these three negatives Sean decided to use a consumer statement. Under the Fair Credit Reporting Act, every American has the right to add a statement of up to 100 words. It can be used to clarify or explain any items and appears on all subsequent reports requested by grantors of credit. Sean had learned that such statements had been useful in representing consumers' cases on a variety of issues.

Sean submitted the following consumer statement: "Our family suffered large, uninsured, and unexpected medical expenses in 2004. Prior to that time we had always paid our creditors promptly. Since that time we have recovered and now pay all of our creditors promptly."

Sean's good work at clearing his credit report and explaining his situation paid off. Within two years he qualified for a home loan. He and Carmen purchased a two-bedroom townhouse in a nice neighborhood populated with couples their age. They enjoyed their new house and appreciated everything about their new life.

How to File a Dispute

Picture the customer service department of a major credit reporting agency. It's large and it's busy. (It may even be based in India instead of the U.S.) It gets thousands of calls and letters each week. Some are legitimate disputes and some are generated with help from credit repair agencies, but it's sometimes hard to know which are which. Some letters from consumers are clear and easy to understand, while some are indecipherable, rambling, and pages long.

Each complaint is handled by a customer service rep with one job: to keep the work moving. He or she will enter the dispute in the computer with a summary code of why the consumer is disputing the information. At the press of a button, that will be fired off to the creditor to be verified. The whole process of entering the dispute usually takes about one minute, and from there it's handled mainly by computer.

What does this mean for you? First of all, it means you shouldn't expect that someone is going to read the entire five-page-long letter you've written about why the information in your report should be changed. It also means that you have to make sure your complaint will work for you and not against you. How do you do that?

The law that governs credit bureaus is called the federal Fair Credit Reporting Act, which was updated by the Fair and Accurate Credit Transactions

Act. It gives you the right to dispute information on your credit report that is inaccurate or incomplete, and requires the lender or credit bureau receiving your dispute to investigate.

If you want to ask the credit bureau to investigate something that appears to be wrong on your credit report, you have the choice of either writing to or calling the credit bureau.

Calling can be faster—if you can get through to someone who can help you. If you call, make sure you take good notes about what was discussed, when, and with whom. And before you call, make sure you can summarize your dispute clearly and in one or two sentences, just as you would if you were writing the bureau. Examples:

- I never held this account.
- This account was not late as listed.
- This account was discharged in my bankruptcy and should list a zero balance.

Written correspondence takes a little longer but leaves a paper trail, which can be much more helpful. (Keep copies.) You'll also avoid getting dragged into a conversation where something you say can be misinterpreted. Many credit repair experts advise that you write, rather than call, but for a straightforward mistake or two you may just want to pick up the phone.

Write your letter by hand *if* your handwriting is neat and legible. (Computer-generated disputes can look like they came from a credit repair company, which credit reporting agencies don't like at all.) Date everything. Include your name, address, Social Security number, and the credit report number if you have one.

Keep it simple. State exactly what's wrong, and what should be listed. Make sure that information stands out in your letter. (See our sample dispute letters in Appendix B for examples.)

If you have proof of your side of the story, include it. *Never* send originals, only copies. And only send documents that are really relevant. Trust me, no one is going to read your whole stack of paperwork.

Send your letters certified mail, return receipt requested and keep copies in your file. You should expect a reply within thirty days.

☞ *Credit Maximizer Tip:* Don't bother filing a dispute with any of the major credit bureaus if you haven't recently ordered your report from that bureau, or from a company that supplies that bureau's report. For example, if you get your report from TransUnion and discover mistakes, you'll need to order your report from Equifax and Experian before you try to file disputes with them. They may not have the same information, and you'll need their correct contact information to make sure your dispute is handled promptly and properly.

I can't emphasize enough how important it is to keep track of all your dealings with the credit bureaus! Create a file and note every phone call, and keep copies of *all* correspondence you send and receive.

The credit reporting agency usually has thirty days to investigate your dispute. If you provide information to back up your side of the story, they must share that with the furnisher (lender, court, or collection agency, for example) that supplied that information.

The furnisher then must review the item and respond to the credit reporting agency, either by noting the item is correct as it's reported, or by making a correction. If the furnisher determines that the item is wrong, it must send a correction to all bureaus that have been given the wrong item.

If the item in question is incomplete, the credit reporting agency must update it. For example, if your report shows a charge-off but does not show that you paid it off, that information must be corrected upon your request.

When the credit reporting agency has completed its reinvestigation, it must supply you with a written response (either that the information is confirmed as correct, or that a change has been made) and must give you a free copy of your credit report reflecting any changes made. If no changes are made, you won't be given your report.

Important: If a correction is made, the credit reporting agency is not supposed to report the deleted item again unless the furnisher first verifies that the item is accurate and complete, *and* the agency notifies you in writing before it reinserts it for a second time. This notice should include the name, address, and phone number of the furnisher.

Note: You can ask the credit bureau to send a corrected report to anyone who received your incorrect report in the last two years for employment purposes, or in the last six months for any other reason. This may not do a whole lot of good if you already were denied credit, insurance, or employment based on mistakes in your report but it probably won't hurt.

Finally, be nice. Think about what it must be like to work at the credit bureau and handle calls and letters from upset consumers day in and day out. If you're on the phone and can't get anywhere with the person you are speaking with, ask for a supervisor. When you're writing your letter, at least be nice, even if you must be firm.

Don't give up!

Getting Answers

If you get your credit report and don't understand something on it, the FCRA gives you the right to contact the credit reporting agency to ask questions. It also requires each of the major credit reporting bureaus to establish a toll-free telephone number, at which people who can answer questions are available during normal business hours. You're supposed to get this toll-free number with any credit report you order from the agencies. But that doesn't always work the way it should.

In fact, the major credit reporting agencies have had to pay fines totaling more than $2.5 million as part of settlements negotiated by the Federal Trade Commission because they did *not* maintain toll-free telephone numbers with personnel who were accessible to consumers during normal business hours.

According to the FTC's complaints, Equifax, TransUnion, and Experian blocked millions of calls from consumers who wanted to discuss the contents and possible errors in their credit reports and kept some of those consumers on hold for unreasonably long periods of time. If you have trouble reaching someone to discuss your credit report, it's a good idea to file a complaint with the FTC at www.ftc.gov.

Credit Bureau or Creditor?

Most people assume that if something is wrong on their credit report, they should notify the credit bureaus to make a correction. But that's not necessarily the case.

When the federal Fair Credit Reporting Act was first written in the 1970s no mention was made of the lenders (called "furnishers" in the act) who reported information to credit bureaus. Trying to get them to correct mistakes then could be like pulling teeth—if you could get them to respond at all.

It got a little better when the FCRA was updated in 1996. The revised law said that anyone who furnishes information to a credit reporting agency cannot report information it "knows or consciously avoids knowing" is inaccurate.

At the end of 2003, Congress amended the Fair Credit Reporting Act with the Fair and Accurate Credit Transactions Act of 2003. FACTA included more detailed requirements for companies that report information. It also now gives consumers the right to dispute mistakes directly with the lenders reporting them.

While the FTC and banking regulators are still working out the details as of this writing, the basic way it will work is this:

You have the right to dispute information directly with a furnisher (lender). If you dispute wrong information directly with the furnisher, it must notify the credit reporting agencies that the information is under dispute. This is important, and you may need to remind them of that in your correspondence.

If you dispute information directly with the furnisher, you should put your dispute in writing and include any documentation you have to back up your side of the story. (If you can get someone on the phone who can help you, that's fine, but often all you'll have is a PO box for an address.) The furnisher then has thirty days to get back to you with the results of its investigation.

The furnisher doesn't have to investigate if it determines your dispute is frivolous or irrelevant, or if it's substantially the same as one you've already submitted *directly to the credit bureau*. It also does not have to investigate if your dispute is initiated by a credit repair company. It does have to tell you why it won't investigate, however, and can't simply choose not to respond.

There are several advantages of filing a dispute directly with the furnisher:

- It probably doesn't get as many disputes as the credit bureaus, and may have information in its files that back up your contention that it's wrong.
- If it makes a correction, it will have to notify *all* the bureaus that have the mistake.
- It's supposed to be careful not to report the same mistake again.

At the same time, the furnisher may not be as efficient as the credit bureau in handling disputes. If it's a collection agency, in particular, it may do a poor job of investigating disputes. Collection agencies assume that everyone who disputes a debt is just trying to wiggle out of it.

In the case of bankruptcy, a tax lien, or a judgment, the furnisher will be a court and you'll have to find out which court has the information. This can be excruciatingly difficult, but stick with it. If the information is wrong, it shouldn't be reported any more than any other wrong information. (The credit reporting agency should give you the name and contact information for the court reporting the information.)

The big problem: Here's what's likely to be the biggest problem with disputing information directly with the furnisher under the new law. The updated FCRA specifically says just the fact that a consumer says the information is wrong is *not* enough to give the furnisher reasonable cause to believe it's inaccurate. The fact of the matter is, however, consumers often find damaging information on their credit reports that they can't *prove* is wrong—they just know it is!

Example: Maria Rodriguez has a collection account from a major retailer on her credit report. She never opened an account with that store. She believes it probably belongs to someone else by the same name. But how can she prove it's not hers? So far, she's spent hours trying to unsuccessfully get the credit bureaus and creditors to remove it.

When you file a dispute with the credit bureau, it also generally has thirty days to investigate and get back to you. If the information can't be verified it must be dropped. (In fact, that's one of the common approaches of the credit repair companies—to just dispute it and hope it gets removed because no one verifies it.) Also, if you find more than one mistake on your report, you can dispute both in the same letter to the credit bureau, which can save you some time.

The disadvantage of going this route is that you'll have to file your dispute with each of the three major credit reporting agencies that have the wrong data, and your dispute isn't likely to be investigated in depth. There are plenty of situations where consumers have disputed information, and even included proof, but gotten nowhere.

Here's the main reason, however, why you want to file a dispute with the credit grantor first. Under the new updated law, if you first dispute the information with the credit bureau and it comes back and says it's correct, then the furnisher can refuse to investigate a second time. That's not true, though, if you start with the furnisher, then try the credit bureau.

☞ *Credit Maximizer Tip:* If you're trying to get wrong information removed from your credit report, dispute it with the credit grantor first. If that doesn't resolve it, then try the credit bureaus.

Disputing Correct Information

There's no magic wand to clean your credit report if it's shot, but there are several things you can do if your credit report is correct but not good. Here are your options:

Just wait: As the information gets older, it becomes less important. As I explained in the last chapter, eventually it will all fall off your report (except unpaid tax liens, which can remain forever).

Rebuild anyway: Take the first strategy of waiting a step further and start adding new positive references to outweigh the old. Understand something here: It's *not* enough to get negative information off your report. You must have positive references to build new, good credit. Someone with no credit history (or a skimpy one) will have a low credit score, just like someone with a negative one.

If you have only one or two (or no) open available credit cards or loans, add some new references. See the section "Building Credit" later in this chapter.

Dispute it: You can always try disputing negative information with the credit bureaus. If it can't be verified, the credit bureaus must remove it. This can be effective in the case of old debts where the furnisher may no longer have easy access to its records. Watch out, though, they may add it on again if it's later verified. (The bureaus are supposed to warn you first in writing, but it doesn't often happen.)

Ask for forgiveness: One way to get accurate but negative information off your report is to ask the creditor to "re-age" the account. By re-aging the account the creditor agrees to remove the late payment(s).

This works best when the account has been paid on time for a good stretch but there were a few late payments with good explanations (illness, move, *perhaps* divorce). Don't bother to ask a creditor to re-age an account with lots of late payments over a long period of time unless you have a really good reason for it.

According to guidelines by the Federal Financial Institutions Examinations Council, creditors should not re-age accounts more than once a year, or twice in five years. The account should be at least nine months old, the borrower should show they are willing and able to pay, and they should make at least three payments in a row on time.

Your challenge will be finding someone who will actually help you at the lender's office, and then convincing them to do so. I recommend you be very patient and polite—after all, you are asking for a favor. But also be persistent. If one person can't help you, ask for a supervisor. If necessary, call back another day. Remember what they say about the squeaky wheel!

Get help: If you have multiple negative items, you may be tempted to try a credit repair company. Sometimes this can be a helpful route to go but be careful. Before you choose one, see our warnings later in this chapter.

Because an accurate credit report is so important, I want to review the rules here for disputes:

1. Make your letter brief (fewer than 100 words).
2. Handwrite your letter when possible. (Be sure your writing is clear and legible.)
3. Keep records of all phone calls, if applicable.
4. Keep copies of all correspondence.
5. Send your letters certified mail, return receipt requested.
6. Dispute inaccuracies with lenders first, then the credit bureaus.
7. Be polite, but persistent.

Getting Nowhere

What happens if you have a legitimate dispute and can't get anywhere with your dispute?

Example: Shana bought a car from a dealer in what turned out to be a scam. As the investigation heated up, she stopped paying the loan on advice from the state attorney general's office, which even provided a letter stating that the information should not appear on her credit file. But her repeated calls and letters to the credit bureau got her nowhere.

You have a few options:

• **Complain to the Federal Trade Commission** at www.ftc.gov. Under the new credit reporting law, if you've tried unsuccessfully to resolve the dispute with the credit bureau, you can file a complaint with the FTC. They will forward each of those complaints to the credit bureaus involved and ask for a response.

• **Hire an attorney.** Not many attorneys take on FCRA cases because the FCRA makes it difficult to win these cases and get any kind of damages. But you may be able to at least hire one to write a few letters for you.

• **Add a statement to your file.** You're allowed a 100-word statement that describes your side of the story. While useful, note that the credit scores don't take those statements into account, and it's often your score that matters.

Building Credit

I've told you how important it is to build good credit. But if you have no credit, or damaged credit, it's tough to get started. Here are a couple of strategies that work well:

• **Get a secured credit card:** A major credit card can be your best friend when it comes to your credit report—if you pay it on time. You can get a secured Visa or MasterCard by putting up a security deposit, usually $200 to $500 to start, with a company that offers the secured card. Use it just like any other major credit card and you'll build your credit. Just make sure it's reported to all three major credit bureaus or it won't be very useful. See the Resources section for more information.

• **Borrow someone else's good credit.** Find someone you trust, who has a sterling credit history, to help you out here. Ask them not to co-sign, but to add you onto their major credit card as an authorized user. You don't ever have to touch the card they'll send. (In fact, it's better you don't or you may be tempted to run up bills you can't pay!)

If the issuer will report your authorized user status to the credit re-porting agencies (and most will) it will appear along with the entire ac-count history for that card. So, suddenly, you can have a ten-year history of a major card paid on time. Just don't abuse the privilege. Don't use the card, and after you've built your credit history ask the person who helped you out to remove you. A warning: If *they* should pay late, *your* credit will be hurt.

Once you have these accounts under your belt for four to six months, then go ahead and get a retail credit card. After another four to six months, go ahead and add another credit reference. And in another four to six months, add a third reference such as another major credit card or an auto loan. Your goal is to have four or five positive references always paid on time—and as little bad debt as possible.

You may not rebuild overnight, but you can see *significant* improvement in your score in as little as six to eighteen months if you stick with it.

Credit Repair Companies

You may have seen ads promising that you can get a brand-new credit file, regardless of your past credit history. Or you may have seen warnings from consumer protection agencies that say that credit repair is a scam. The truth probably lies somewhere in between.

Credit repair agencies do generate *lots* of complaints to the Federal Trade Commission and other agencies that protect consumers. In 1998, for example, the FTC filed thirty-one cases against credit repair firms as part of Operation Eraser—a federal-state crackdown on fraudulent credit repair companies. And in 2000, the FTC put over 180 Web sites on notice that their credit repair claims may violate state and federal laws.

Why do people fall victim to credit repair? The biggest reason is they are desperate to borrow again. Their credit has already been ruined and now they are looking for another way to borrow. Throwing your money away on credit repair so you can just get more bad debt is not a wise investment.

But another reason people want to repair their credit is that they've made mistakes and now they want to start building wealth. Access to credit at decent rates for good debt can help. That's a good reason to want to rebuild your credit, but it's not a reason to waste money on phony credit repair schemes.

Let's look at the truth about credit repair.

MYTH #1: WE CAN SHOW YOU HOW TO GET A BRAND-NEW CREDIT RATING

These ads are typically touting one of several scams. One is to steal the identities of people who have died, sometimes in far-off places like Puerto Rico or Guam, and use them to get credit. Authorities in Georgia, for example, uncovered a fraud ring that sold identities of deceased people for $500 to $600 apiece. The fraudsters scanned obituaries and then ordered background checks—including Social Security numbers and credit reports of the people who had died—over the Internet. Eighty people were suspected to be involved in the crime, in which they then used these recently deceased people as "co-signers" on auto loans.

Another variation is to offer to teach people to build a brand-new credit identity. This scam is called "file segregation." One technique they teach is to get an employer identification number, or EIN, which is similar in digits to a

Social Security number. The idea then is to try to set up a whole new credit file under the EIN.

Here's what the Federal Trade Commission says about file segregation: "It is a federal crime to make any false statements on a loan or credit application. The credit repair company may advise you to do just that. It is a federal crime to misrepresent your Social Security number. It also is a federal crime to obtain an EIN from the IRS under false pretenses. Further, you could be charged with mail or wire fraud if you use the mail or the telephone to apply for credit and provide false information. Worse yet, file segregation likely would constitute civil fraud under many state laws."

But here's the real reason to just say no. It can be difficult to effectively start a credit history—even with a new Social Security number or employer identification number. By the time you've gone to that much trouble you might as well have just worked on rebuilding your credit in legitimate ways. Save your money and do it the right way.

MYTH #2: WE CAN GET YOU CREDIT, GUARANTEED

If you're having trouble getting credit, you may be drawn to companies that promise they can get you a major credit card or line of credit, guaranteed. The hitch is that they charge a fee, maybe just $100, or maybe as much as $1,000 or more. Under the Telemarketing Sales Rule, if someone guarantees or suggests that there is a strong chance they can get or arrange a loan or other form of credit for you, it's against the law to ask you to pay—or accept payment—for their service until you get your loan or credit.

Here's another "guaranteed credit card" rip-off. A credit card advertised heavily on the Internet promises a "$7,500 Unsecured Platinum Credit Line." In small print below, it says "for all kinds of our merchandise." This is a modern version of the "catalogue cards" that were marketed in the late 1980s and early 1990s. You get a credit card and can use it to purchase merchandise out of that particular companies' catalogue. Now maybe the merchandise is okay and not overpriced. (You can't tell because you don't see the catalogue unless you sign up.) But even so, it costs $149 to sign up and you may have to make a hefty down payment on the merchandise you do buy.

Another variation is a guaranteed credit card with so many fees and charges that you essentially pay several hundred dollars for a credit line of about $50. For example, one card offers a guaranteed credit card. When you read the fine print, about $225 in fees will be charged against a "total" credit line of $300. That means you're paying $225 for a $75 line of credit. A secured card, where you will eventually get your deposit back, is obviously a much better deal than that.

MYTH #3: THERE'S NOTHING THAT CREDIT REPAIR FIRMS CAN DO THAT YOU CAN'T DO ON YOUR OWN

While most credit repair is a rip-off, there are times when it can be helpful—if you find a decent credit repair agency to work with (a challenge in itself); for direction to a reputable firm, visit www.successdna.com. If you have a lot of negative items due to a divorce, bankruptcy, and so on, or if you've been battling the credit bureaus or creditors with no success, you may need a company that has experience in working with those kinds of problems.

Just as you can do your own taxes or hire someone else to prepare them, there are times when it makes sense to hire a credit repair firm to take on the tedious task of correcting your file.

Unfortunately, the FCRA makes it so difficult to sue creditors or credit bureaus that most attorneys won't even take them on. There are law firms that specialize in credit repair, but some have gotten in trouble with the FTC so choose carefully.

YOU HAVE RIGHTS

Credit repair companies are regulated by federal law, and in many cases, state laws. Under the federal Credit Repair Organizations Act, credit repair companies must give you a copy of the "Consumer Credit File Rights Under State and Federal Law" disclosure before you sign a contract. They also must give you a written contract that spells out your rights and obligations. Read the contract!

You have specific protections under that law. For example, a credit repair company cannot:

- Make false claims about their services;
- Perform any services until they have your signature on a written contract and have completed a three-day waiting period. During this time, you can cancel the contract without paying any fees; or
- Charge you until they have completed the promised services.

Many of the credit repair firms get around the up-front money clause by charging a fee for educational services, then performing the credit repair. Many will refund fees if they can't successfully remove items from your file.

Please be careful about spending your money on credit repair. There are so many rip-offs out there that it's important you check out any company carefully, and consider what you can do on your own.

Chapter XII

Common Credit Report Problems

Here are some of the common problems on credit reports that trip people up and what you can do about them.

Joint and Co-signed Accounts

You co-signed a credit card or loan for your boyfriend, co-worker, or ex. Now they've defaulted and you're stuck with the bad credit. If you agreed to the account when it was opened, it's accurate and you have to deal with it as accurate information (see below).

Example: Sara co-signed on a Visa card for her daughter when she went to college. Since her daughter always paid the bills on time, she forgot about it. Within several years, Sara's daughter had gotten married and was now getting divorced. In the meantime, she had also added her husband to the account. He ran up large bills and ran off without paying them. Sara's credit was trashed along with her daughter's.

If you've co-signed a credit card and don't want to be part of it anymore, at least get the account closed to new future charges. Don't let the creditor bully you into thinking you need the other person's consent to do that. (Sometimes they say they won't close it out without both parties' consent.) If necessary, get an attorney to write a letter stating you want the account closed and won't be responsible for any new charges. Doing this won't remove the account from your credit report, but it could protect you from *future* late payments.

Authorized Users

If you've ever asked your credit card issuer to send you a card for your spouse or child, you've requested an authorized user on your account. An authorized user is different from a joint account holder in that they don't sign for (or agree to) the account. So they are not legally responsible for the bills, but they are entitled to use the account. If you do add someone else to your account as an authorized user, you'll be stuck with any charges they make, so be careful!

If the authorized user is a spouse, the Equal Credit Opportunity Act requires lenders to report the account in both names to credit bureaus. Watch out if you have an authorized user (or are one) and are going through divorce, bankruptcy, or other problems that can affect your credit. Get your name off the account quickly if you think the other person may have problems paying it on time.

If you were an authorized user on an account that went bad, ask the lender to remove the account from your credit history since you weren't responsible legally for it. Again, here's where you have to be persistent.

Divorce

Divorce can be tough enough without having to deal with the effects of a ruined credit rating. The most common scenario is that the judge assigns joint accounts to one spouse in the divorce decree. The other spouse figures they are off the hook. But the divorce decree does not erase the original contract with the creditor. Joint accounts can still be reported on your credit report—seven years for negative information and indefinitely for positive information.

Most creditors would much rather have two people to collect from than one, so they are unwilling to remove a spouse from a co-signed account. But some consumers have been successful in persuading creditors to remove from their credit reports accounts that were assigned to their ex in divorce. It doesn't hurt to try. The exception? If your ex is currently behind on one of the joint accounts, contacting the creditor or collection agency could mean they'll start coming after *you*.

Tangled Webs

Denny and Lyn were star-crossed lovers. Their friends all felt that the universe would have been a much better place if they had never met. Like a black hole, the two sucked all light and reasonable matter into a vortex of inescapable weight and gravity. And just as black holes aren't much fun for planets, Denny and Lyn weren't much fun for the friends and family in their orbit.

It all started out innocently enough. Denny was the star halfback at a small Southern college. Lyn was the prettiest, most popular cheerleader. They were destined to at least date each other.

Denny was a prolific yard gainer for his Division II school but realized he didn't have the size to make it into the pros. It didn't matter. On top of his athletic ability, charm, and good looks, Denny had a brain. He excelled in science and was admitted to medical school in the Northwest. He breezed through the rigors of the training and found his calling, becoming a gynecologist.

Lyn followed Denny to the Northwest. While he was studying day and night she had nothing to do. Lyn too, in addition to good looks and a winning manner, had a brain. She decided to continue her education while she waited for Denny to ask her to get married. She applied to the school's law school and was promptly accepted.

In what seemed like a flash Denny was a board-certified gynecologist and Lyn was a licensed attorney. They were both attractive, well-educated, and polished: the perfect couple. Marriage was inevitable.

Two children, a perfect boy and a perfect girl, soon followed, as did larger houses and nicer cars. They were ever more successful in their respective fields.

Eventually, the mix of success and money, good looks and active synapses started to make for a destructive brew. Denny and Lyn could get whatever they wanted. Whether with their looks or their power or their money or all of them combined there were no restrictions on them. And with no restrictions the bounds of morality, humility, and discretion that others feel did not apply. Denny and Lyn were free to take whatever they wanted. Denny ended up cheating with a patient named Laura. Lyn cheated with a partner at her firm.

And so events were put into motion.

Friends told friends who told more friends and soon everyone knew of the double infidelity.

Denny moved out. It didn't work out with Laura. She claimed he misused his position as a doctor. The state medical board was investigating this serious charge. Denny was undeterred and soon was seeing a parade of former patients.

The partner's wife found out. Her family owned a company that was a large and powerful client of the firm. The company threatened to take their legal work elsewhere unless Lyn was fired by the firm.

Lyn was fired.

Denny and Lyn blamed each other for their sudden change in fortune. A nasty and very public divorce ensued. Friends and family were forced to take sides. Friendships were lost. The ripple effect of the divorce far exceeded the lives of the two parents and two children. It was destructive and unavoidable and left many good people wishing the two had never married.

When the bitter and expensive proceedings were all over the court split things roughly in half anyway. Lyn ended up with the house. Because their earning power was almost equal the court awarded Lyn with $5,000 a month in child support payments with Denny receiving weekend visitation rights.

Being fired by her firm made finding another job difficult for Lyn. She was now damaged goods in the rarefied world of large law firms. She thought about going out on her own but was honestly tired of practicing law. After all the firm politics and client demands she needed a break. She recalled the old lawyer's joke that the best practice was one without clients. With the $5,000 a month she was getting from Denny she thought she could make the house payment and take care of the kids.

But she couldn't. Her expenses ran about $6,000 a month, especially now that she was dating the pool man, who was in his early thirties and needed to be kept happy.

Lyn reasoned that Denny owed her even more money to take care of his children. She applied for a new joint credit card using both of their financial information. Of course, Lyn knew all of Denny's particulars. And because she wasn't working, his employment history certainly helped secure the high-limit credit card.

Lyn took care of the children but she also was having some fun. When Denny had the kids on the weekend she and the pool man would fly to San Francisco to shop or Reno to ski. They were enjoyable and expensive sojourns.

Soon Lyn fell behind on the house payments. She wasn't worried. Denny's attorney had forgotten to address the issue during the nasty divorce. Her counsel had told her what she already knew as an attorney.

When one party ends up with the house there has to be a requirement in the property settlement agreement that the house either be sold or refinanced. If both parties remain responsible for the mortgage and the spouse awarded the house fails to make the monthly payments the other spouse is still responsible for the loan.

This fact hit Denny like a ton of bricks when he went out shopping for a new house.

After dating a full complement of ladies around town, Denny had fallen for Jennifer, a young, recently divorced mother of two. They had a great deal in common, including incredibly contentious divorce proceedings in the recent past. Unlike Denny's situation, Jennifer's settlement required that the house be sold or refinanced. With Denny needing a place for his two children and now Jennifer's two children it made sense to locate a larger home together.

Denny and Jennifer found the perfect house for their combined four children. It had a big yard and a nice pool. While they would have to find a new pool maintenance company it was otherwise ready to move into and enjoy.

Until Denny learned of his credit problems. Lyn hadn't made the house payment for three months now. It was in pre-foreclosure proceedings. Lyn also had failed to make the payments on the joint credit card she obtained without his knowledge for the last two months.

Denny's credit was in terrible shape. He was not going to be buying a house anytime soon. Jennifer was furious. Denny asked for her understanding.

She had been through a nasty divorce too and he felt she should appreciate his situation. But she didn't. She needed a house for her children. She demanded that they get Denny's credit straightened out immediately.

Denny and Jennifer met with a local attorney specializing in credit issues. Denny first wanted to know if he could buy his old house in pre-foreclosure. It had appreciated greatly and if he could pick it up he could make some good money.

Jennifer bristled at the idea. She didn't want him anywhere near the old house.

Before Denny could get angry the attorney informed them that because the house was several months behind in payments, the lender had called the entire balance due. If Denny wanted his house back, he needed to get his credit straightened out. The attorney stated that the first issue to be dealt with was the joint credit card that Lyn had taken out without Denny's permission. The attorney suggested the proper way to handle it was for Denny to file a police report on the fraudulent activity. It was only with a police report that the credit card company would investigate the matter and ultimately remove the negative credit scores from Denny's credit report.

Denny said he couldn't file a police report on Lyn. She was the mother of his children, and she took care of them 80 percent of the time. He wasn't going to have his children raised by a felon.

With this Jennifer blew. It was either Lyn or her. Denny again asked for her understanding, but Jennifer got up and walked out of the office.

Denny and the attorney sat for a moment in stunned silence. When Denny started to laugh with relief, the attorney knew why and had to chuckle himself.

Together they worked out a plan to restore Denny's credit. It involved tapping into some of Denny's retirement plans, paying some penalties for early withdrawals and using the cash to get him clean. They paid off Lyn's credit card and shut the card down. The card issuer agreed to re-age the account and remove the late payments in exchange for Denny's full payment. They also arranged a workout agreement with the lender that brought the house payment current, then petitioned the court to require Lyn to sell or refinance it.

Lyn was shaken by these moves back into a mode of responsibility. Ditching the pool man, she found a low-stress, reasonably paying job with a public interest legal group. She sold the expensive mansion she didn't really need and found a nice home in a decent neighborhood with good schools for the children.

Denny was able to straighten out his credit issues in a short period of time. He had the satisfaction of knowing he had avoided a second certain divorce and that his children weren't raised by a felon.

☞ *Credit Maximizer Tip:* If you are separating it is essential that you:

1. Close joint accounts to further charges.
2. Stipulate that your ex will refinance the house or sell it within a certain time period, if you are both on the note.
3. Transfer any joint balances to individual accounts if at all possible.
4. Monitor your credit report monthly for fraud or future problems.

Marriage

Some financial experts advise showing each other your credit report before you say "I do." It's not bad advice. At a minimum, understand what marriage does to your credit. If you have separate credit together before you marry, there's no reason to join all of it.

Simply getting married won't merge your credit history. You'll have to add your new spouse to your accounts or vice versa for them to be reported on both your credit reports.

Here is an example: Justin and Kayla are getting married. She has a few student loans, always paid on time, and just one credit card. He's already trashed his credit. If she adds him onto her accounts, she runs the risk that he'll run up bills that she'll be stuck with. If he adds her to his accounts, she'll instantly be saddled with those negative accounts on her credit history. A low-limit joint account they open together may be their safest bet—if she wants to take even that risk.

My advice is to maybe have one joint account you use for joint household purchases but keep the rest separate. Of course, your auto loans or mortgage may be joint debts, but they don't necessarily have to be. If one of you needs to build a better credit rating, you can try the strategy of "borrowing" their good credit that we describe under the section "Building Credit."

☞ *Credit Maximizer Tip:* Watch out in community property states (Arizona, California, Idaho, Louisiana, Nevada, New Mexico, Texas, Washington, and Wisconsin) because in those states all debt incurred by each spouse *during* the marriage may become part of the community property—meaning you could get stuck with his or her bills. Even then, however, your *individual* accounts will not be reported on your spouse's credit report or vice versa.

Here's a problem that can come up when a spouse or ex-spouse files bankruptcy. Any joint accounts included in the bankruptcy may be listed on the credit report as included in bankruptcy. Due to a lawsuit a few years back, the credit bureaus have changed their system to search and find out whether the spouse who didn't file was involved in the bankruptcy. If not, the bureaus say they will not list the bankruptcy on the "innocent" spouse's credit report. But creditors may still do so if the couple are not careful.

Example: Kevin filed for bankruptcy but his wife, Marta, did not. They had a joint retail credit card that had not been used for some time and was not included in the bankruptcy. Because Kevin filed, however, the card issuer closed the account and reported it on both credit reports as "included in bankruptcy" even though it wasn't. Marta had to ask the card issuer to remove the bankruptcy from her credit report since it wasn't accurate.

Death

If you had joint accounts with someone who died, then you will be responsible for the bills. If you live in a community property state and your spouse dies, you will be responsible for all debt incurred during the marriage. If you were an authorized user on your parents' or spouse's account (not in a community property state) or you were not on the accounts at all, you are *not* responsible for those bills. This includes parents whose college student children obtained their own credit cards without a parent co-signer.

The creditor may try to collect from the estate, if there is any. Whether they will do so depends on the size of the debt and whether the creditor believes they can succeed. Don't be pressured into paying those bills directly, especially if it will hurt your family financially!

Warning: Credit card issuers will sometimes try to use guilt or even trick children, spouses, or parents into paying the individual bills of the deceased. They may falsely tell the survivor that the debt is their responsibility. Or they will offer to "transfer" the balance to a new account in their name. In one appalling situation, a college student committed suicide after running up large debts, and the card issuers hounded his mother to pay those bills for a couple of years later. If you run into this situation, don't agree to anything until you contact an attorney. You may also want to consider complaining to the banking regulators and/or your state attorney general's office.

Mixed Up

You may find accounts you don't recall ever owning. It's possible that through a bank merger or the sale of some accounts, your account went to a new lender and you just don't recognize the name of the new lender. Or it's possible they have you mixed up with someone else—especially if you have a common name. Contact the creditor to clarify it. Worst-case scenario: An account you don't recognize could signal identity theft.

Old Balances

The balance that's reported on an account to the credit bureau is that balance reported on the day the creditor sends its data to the bureau. If you pay off your account in full each month, the zero balance may not be reflected depending on when the balance is reported. When you pay off an account completely, it can take up to forty-five days or so to actually show up on your credit report.

If you have an account that was charged off, it may show a balance until it is paid or settled. A paid tax lien or collection account should show a zero balance.

If you've paid off an account at least three months ago and the report still lists a balance, by all means dispute it.

Example: Richard travels internationally for business. He has an American Express card that he uses for those purposes. His monthly travel expenses are sometimes as high as $10,000 to $20,000, which he pays in full when he is re-imbursed. His credit report shows high "balances" on those accounts even though he pays in full.

Unauthorized Inquiries

It's difficult to get inquiries removed. The main reason is that the FCRA *requires* credit bureaus to show you the names of companies that have inquired into your credit for the last year (two years for employment inquiries). Even if a review of your report wasn't authorized, the fact remains that someone accessed your file and the bureau is supposed to tell you that.

If you have multiple unauthorized inquiries on your report—if you're a fraud victim in particular—you can ask the credit bureau to *block* those inquiries. If they are blocked, no one will see them but you and they won't affect your credit score. If you have a few inquiries you didn't expect, however, you'll have to decide if it's worth the time or trouble to try to dispute them.

Bankruptcy

When you file bankruptcy, the bankruptcy is listed, as well as each of the accounts included in bankruptcy. While bankruptcy can offer a "fresh start" from debts it does *not* wipe out the original accounts that appeared on your report. If an account was charged off in bankruptcy, for example, it may be listed as a "charge-off" or "profit-and-loss" account, but it shouldn't show a balance if your bankruptcy is completed. If it does, dispute it and include a copy of your list of your discharged debts from your bankruptcy papers as proof.

If your bankruptcy is dismissed or withdrawn, it will still be reported for the same length of time as if you had gone through with it.

Again, while all bankruptcies may be reported for ten years from the date you filed, major credit bureaus will remove Chapter 13 bankruptcies seven years from the filing date.

Auto Repossessions

When your car is repo'd, the repossession will be listed on your credit report and remain for seven years from the date of repossession. If you turn in the keys, it's called a voluntary repossession and may appear on your report for the same length of time as a regular repossession, unless you can negotiate something different with the lender.

Another warning: In most states, your vehicle will be sold at auction and if the price it brings is less than the balance on the loan (plus legal repossession costs, attorney's fees, or other costs that may apply), you can be sued for the deficiency. A deficiency judgment may then be awarded by the court and also appear on your credit report.

Released Judgments or Tax Liens

Even though your tax lien was released or your judgment was paid, it won't automatically be removed. As we explained in the previous chapter they can still be reported after they've been paid. But if you don't pay them, they can remain on your credit file for a long, long time.

Simply paying a judgment or tax lien won't likely improve your credit score. It will, however, start the clock ticking so that item will eventually get removed.

Credit Counseling

While entering a credit counseling program does affect your credit, it may not be as bad as you think. First, most creditors will re-age your accounts once you enter the program and make three on-time payments. That means they'll erase those immediate late payments before you entered the program.

For those that do report the account as being paid through credit counseling, the FICO score won't take that into account in calculating your credit score.

Your credit cards, however, will be closed during the program so it will be unlikely you can get new loans. Also, many mortgage lenders will view a credit counseling program as very negative. There are lenders, though, that understand the value of credit counseling and will be willing to finance a loan once you have been successfully paying on your program for at least one or two years, provided you meet their other requirements.

Warning: If the counseling agency pays your creditors late, you will be responsible for those bills and will be stuck with the late payments on your credit report. This *has* happened, so choose a counseling agency carefully.

Collection Accounts

Collection accounts are tricky and they deserve their own section here. A collection account is automatically considered negative information, so *simply paying it may not make a significant difference in your credit score*.

There are usually two accounts reported in the case of a collection account: the original account with the lender and the collection account. The exception would be when the original creditor (cell phone company, medical provider, or whoever) doesn't regularly report to the credit bureaus. In those cases, just the collection account will be listed.

If more than one collection account is reported for the same debt because you didn't pay and it was turned over to another collection agency, only the most recent collection account should be listed.

Details about the original account are much more important than details on the collection account, simply because the collection account is automatically negative, and as I've explained, paying off a collection account, in and of itself, will not likely help your credit score.

If you do have an account that was reported on your credit report—say a major credit card—that was then sent to collection, the original creditor may not be willing to discuss or negotiate with you. If they will, however, it's usually better to work with a creditor than a collection agency.

If the collection account is not paid, the creditor or collection agency has a number of years—based on the state statute of limitations—to sue you for the debt. Clearly you don't want a lawsuit on your credit report, but before they sue you, you must be notified they are taking you to court and you may then have an opportunity to negotiate a payoff with them. If the statute of limitations has expired, then you can't be sued for the debt and there's not much they can do to collect from you.

A collection account, as we mentioned earlier, can only be reported seven and a half years from the date you originally missed your payment. Even if you don't pay it, it cannot be reported longer. If a collection agency tells you otherwise, keep notes. Stating that the information can remain longer than it legally can, or that the collector "has ways" to keep it on the report longer, could be a violation of the Fair Debt Collection Practices Act, which doesn't allow false statements.

Here are some things you should consider as far as your credit report is concerned:

• Are you likely to get sued for the debt? If so, paying it will prevent a court judgment on your credit report if you lose your case. Of course, it's tough to know when a creditor or collection agency is telling the truth about suing you.

• Can you get the collection agency to *remove* the account from your credit file if you pay it off? If they agree, you must get this in writing from them first *before* you pay. Collection agencies often promise the moon, but don't do a thing once they've been paid. Note: They can't do anything about the account with the original creditor, which may be *more* important to your credit.

• If you negotiate a payoff of less than the full amount, your account will be listed as "settled" for less than the full amount and that will be considered negative.

• Is it an old debt that either can't be reported anymore, or will fall off your credit report soon anyway? Consumers have complained that collection agencies say they'll report debts that are older than ten or more years. That's illegal.

• What does the original account list? If it lists a charge-off with a zero balance, paying if off won't help much. If it lists a charge-off with a balance, and by paying it you can get the original creditor to update the account with a zero balance, then you have a chance at boosting your score a little.

If you're applying for a mortgage, the lender may require you to pay off an outstanding collection account before they'll give you a mortgage. Again, aim to get the collection agency to remove it if at all possible. If not, at least get something in writing stating it's been paid in full.

Remember, collection agencies are supposed to report the date you first fell behind leading up to the collection account. If yours lists an account and that information isn't included, challenge it.

Chapter XIII

Scams

A huge irony exists in the marketplace. The more honest Americans there are struggling with poor credit due to divorce, bankruptcy, medical crisis, or other life-changing event, the more responsible individuals there are who sincerely want to work out their credit issues with integrity and resolve, the more blatant and outrageously fraudulent the scam artists have become in targeting the vulnerable. And the all too frequent result is that a genuine intention to improve one's credit standing is crushed by an unethical operator who only worsens your credit.

How can you avoid being a target for fraud?

First, by reading this chapter and understanding the patterns and come-ons of the scam artists. The scamsters prey on your fears and vulnerabilities. You need to ask yourself: Am I being manipulated? It is not hard to do. Step back from the come-on and rationally analyze whether it was presented in a way that used your fears to manipulate your decision. Try to see through the come-on.

A second way to avoid being a target is to not jump for offers that sound too good to be true. As we all know, offers that seem too good to be true are usually exactly that. The problem is we like the sound of it—"All your credit problems resolved for $199!" or "Guaranteed Credit No Matter What!" This problem's cure has to be pure cynicism. Don't believe a word of any of it until you completely verify and thoroughly check out the problem. And then still be cynical.

After all, if all of us could have our credit problems resolved for only $199 there would be no need to read this book. Heck, there would be no need to even write this book.

But we're reading and writing because there are no panaceas, there are no simple cures. Credit problems can be overcome when dealt with in a realistic and systematic manner. They are rarely, if ever, cured by paying a third party offering the illusory promise of instant redemption.

Brian Sandoval is the attorney general for the state of Nevada. He and a staff of dedicated attorneys work to overcome a myriad of credit repair scams. It is not an easy job.

Nevada and other states require that credit repair companies register and post a bond with the state's Consumer Affairs Division. Under state law companies may not require the payment of monies in advance of services. And yet such protections are no guarantee. Jo Ann Gibbs, a deputy attorney general for consumer fraud in Las Vegas, recounted the case of a credit repair company with a history of legitimate operations. Unfortunately, the company's owner developed a severe gambling addiction and began embezzling the clients' money instead of making the required payments on their debts. The fraud was not detected for some time. When it finally was, the consumers were in much worse shape, with even greater debts and late charges now due, than they were before they signed up with the company.

Sandoval and his staff have also investigated a number of companies offering credit repair services for a fee of between $250 and $500. These services only made matters worse for the unsuspecting consumer. The companies would send out a letter to each of the three credit bureaus simply stating that "the debts were not mine" or using only the word "fraud."

The statements were not only incomplete but usually false as well. Worse yet, by notifying the credit bureau that the consumer may be a fraud victim their account is flagged for review and greater security. The consumer must provide additional information and verification when applying for future credit, and may have more difficulty obtaining credit due to the fraudulent activity reported on his account.

The lesson is to not pay someone $250 to further harm your credit account.

Another scam that the Nevada attorney general's office has investigated involves a credit card come-on for people with bad credit. For a significant amount of money, usually between $299 and $399 (which is directly withdrawn from the consumer's bank account), the scamsters promise a credit card. However, instead of being sent a real credit card, the consumer receives a flimsy pamphlet on credit and an application for a Visa or Master-Card. The consumer is instructed to return the application not to Visa or MasterCard but to the company. The scamsters promise a refund if the consumer's application is rejected for credit three times. This promise is empty and illusory since the application is never actually submitted. Consumer follow-up calls are ignored. The bad guys have already banked the money.

Allowing the direct withdrawal of monies from your bank account presents its own problems . . .

Automatic Problems

Jim was sitting on the couch beaming and fuming. He was beaming over the fact that he had slammed two home runs that afternoon at the company softball game. A few of the worthy secretaries at the annual picnic were eyeing him favorably for the two monster blasts he put over the fence. He felt good about that.

He was fuming because he felt worthless. He had crushed those pitches due to his anger at his financial condition. It seemed like he could never get ahead. Just when everything seemed to be getting better he was doubled up and back on the sidelines.

The latest setback involved his mother and her health. Jim's father had passed away five years ago and hadn't left his mother in the best financial situation. Jim knew his father had intended to do so but there was always another car or vacation or time-share deal to distract him.

Jim's mother had recently had major surgery. She was fine physically but financially the procedure put quite a burden on her. Not wanting her to worry, Jim had taken over the payments. This not only delayed Jim from saving for a house but it severely crimped his monthly budget. He was single and getting older by the day. He wanted to have a family but didn't want to raise children under a financial cloud. And he wasn't getting any nearer to his goal. He had been late on a few bills lately, which greatly bothered him.

Jim figured if he could temporarily get some extra credit all would be fine. And then the phone rang.

The caller asked if Jim would like to qualify for a major credit card. When Jim said he didn't have the best credit the caller said he needn't worry. The card they offered was available regardless of past credit problems.

When Jim indicated an interest the caller promptly asked if he had a checking account. Jim said he did and the caller responded that then they could proceed.

The offer sounded too good to be true. The credit card would allow him some breathing room so he could pay his monthly bills and his mother's medical bills. He felt reasonably positive about getting a raise at work and felt that he could handle the extra interest and principal payments over the next year.

The caller then asked for information necessary to obtain the new credit card. As Jim answered all the questions the caller asked for him to get one of his checks and to read off all the numbers at the bottom. When Jim asked why this information was needed the caller said it was necessary to help ensure that Jim qualified for this outstanding offer. Jim gave out all the requested information and the caller congratulated him on improving his credit.

Jim hung up the phone and went back to thinking about the worthy secretaries eyeing him that day. If he owned his own place they'd like him even more. Home runs were great but a home was even better.

After several weeks Jim wondered what happened to the credit card deal. They were supposed to send him the card within two weeks and he hadn't received anything. He didn't have a number for the company and realized he'd have to wait awhile longer.

Two months later Jim received a notice that his checking account was seriously overdrawn. He couldn't understand why. He hadn't spent money on anything but the basics and his mother's medical bills. How could he be overdrawn?

He called the bank to find out what was wrong. The customer service representative indicated that recently a demand draft had been presented for $150 a week.

Jim said he didn't know what a demand draft was and asked for an explanation. The representative informed him that the demand draft had his name, account information, and amount on it. Unlike a regular check it didn't require a signature. A total of $750 had been paid to this company. Didn't he know about it?

Jim became angry and wanted to know why the bank would allow someone to pull that much money out of his account without his permission.

The representative politely informed him that they didn't do that, and that by submitting the draft with all of his correct information someone did have his permission.

Jim grew angrier and said he had not given any permission to steal money from his account.

The representative was calm. She had been through this before. She asked if Jim had given out his checking account information over the phone to anyone.

Jim then remembered the credit card solicitation call. He was curious at the time why the checking account numbers were needed. Now he knew why.

The bank representative was helpful. She arranged to prevent any further debiting. She gave him the number of their state's attorney general so he could report the fraud and, perhaps, get his money back if the criminals were ever caught. And she confirmed what Jim now knew: Never give out your bank information over the phone.

The automatic debit scam is alive and well in the country. Unscrupulous telemarketers prey on unsuspecting consumers like Jim every day. The promises range from credit cards for those with bad credit to valuable prizes for a select group of winners. All that is needed is some basic information, which during the happy gathering period includes confidential checking account information.

A telltale sign of the scam is when the telemarketer asks in the first minute of the call if you have a checking account. If you don't they will move on to the next potential victim. If you do, they will sell you the sweetest offer to get your information so they can start submitting demand drafts without your signature and raid your account.

Are demand drafts themselves illegal? No. Plenty of people pay their mortgages or their car payments through automatic debiting of their checking account. From a convenience standpoint at the very least it saves a stamp.

But even if you are sure you are working with a reputable company such as Countrywide Mortgage or GMAC you will want to handle the creation of a demand draft withdrawal payment through the mail.

The law allows telemarketers to obtain your authorization to tap your checking account over the phone by obtaining your tape-recorded permission. Do not allow this to happen. Even though the law permits it there is too much room for trickery.

Insist that all permission only be granted in writing and through the mail. Insist that the necessary forms be sent to you. Read them carefully and understand the transaction before you send the forms back.

And remember to never, ever give out your checking account information over the phone.

Platinum or Alchemy?

Another scam that separates you from your money is as follows:

Gwen and Horace lead an interesting life. Gwen had been born and raised in Rhyl, a small Welsh seaport and vacation spot thirty miles west of Liverpool. Her family knew George Harrison's family when she was growing up and she eventually became friends with all of the Beatles as they were starting out in the small clubs around Liverpool.

Gwen had a mind for numbers. In school she could figure out all the math problems in less than an instant. As she grew older she could spot mathematical patterns and inconsistencies with amazing alacrity. Her school counselor wanted her to go into science, mathematics, or perhaps chartered accounting. But the family needed her in their peewee golf/fish and chips enterprise. Naturally, Gwen became the bookkeeper.

Gwen kept up with George and the Beatles as they became worldwide sensations. She'd see them in Liverpool or in Rhyl now and then and was happy for their success. As their band became a business to deal with and their music became an asset to account for, the Fab Four complained about the need to keep track of everything. George knew that Gwen had a mind for numbers and asked if she'd come to London to help with the books. Her family realized it was a great opportunity and so Gwen moved to London and started working for the Beatles' Apple Corp. tracking all the royalty payments.

Royalty statements from publishing and media companies were in the form of hieroglyphics masking misstatements and misrepresentations. They were intentionally vague and difficult to decipher. Ringo wouldn't even look at one. But Gwen learned how to read them and how to challenge them and along the way recovered millions and millions of dollars the band would have otherwise lost. John called her the fifth Beatle.

Gwen met Horace in London during a particularly nasty fight over book royalties. Horace was an American living in England and he represented a larger American publishing house. They had published several Beatle books with great success. The royalties to the band didn't reflect that success. As Gwen tore into their statements Horace became attracted. He had never met such a woman. They were married soon after.

Gwen and Horace settled outside London. Their jobs were challenging and enjoyable and the years passed quickly. Then one day the two of them realized that they had worked hard enough and it was time to retire. Horace was tired of the gray dampness of England and wanted to move to the sunny clime of Florida. Gwen was game. The two traveled to Tampa to investigate.

A house was located in a nice retirement community. A problem arose as they arranged to purchase it.

Neither Gwen nor Horace had any current established American credit. The banks and the credit bureaus didn't know who they were. While they had excellent credit in England it didn't travel with them to the United States. They couldn't finance the house.

Gwen made an executive decision. They would sell their house in England and buy the house in Florida with all cash. They would worry about establishing credit later. Horace agreed, the sellers agreed, and so it happened.

As they settled into their new house in Florida Gwen set about to establish credit. She opened a bank account and asked for a credit card. The bank indicated that she had no credit history and would have to start with a debit card, which the bank didn't offer. Gwen left in a huff. Two other banks said the same thing. Gwen was not pleased.

Later that day she saw a newspaper advertisement for a platinum credit card. The ad promised that participation in the program would lead to a Visa or MasterCard credit card, better credit reports, and many other financial benefits. The platinum card cost $99, which, given Gwen's frustration level, seemed reasonable to pay. The operator suggested they could automatically debit Gwen's checking account. Gwen didn't like that idea and said she would send a check.

In another week the card arrived and Gwen sensed something was wrong. Her bookkeeping and royalty statement/misstatement antenna was up. The platinum card she paid $99 for only allowed her to make credit purchases from a general merchandise catalogue. Plus, the merchandise in the catalogue was almost double the price over what a regular discount store charged. If this card was platinum, Gwen fumed, then alchemy existed.

The materials also described how they obtained credit for you. For another $299 a credit card could be obtained. A deposit of $2,000 was required and with that you could charge up to $1,000. The credit card being so expensively offered was a secured card that only allowed for a 50 percent charge. Then more money had to be deposited. This wasn't a credit card program, Gwen decided; it was a credit card scam.

Now very angry, Gwen called the number listed to complain. It had a 900 prefix, which Gwen assumed was akin to a toll-free 800 line. The line was answered by a recording which indicated that due to call volume she would be on hold for a few minutes. She then heard softened Beatles elevator music, which Gwen fumed the royalties probably weren't being paid on.

After an interminable set of songs Gwen finally got a live operator. She demanded to know if this service was a scam. The operator answered her every question with a question, further frustrating Gwen. After a long and circuitous conversation Gwen was able to cancel the service.

On her next phone bill Gwen learned the meaning of a 900 number. She was billed $3.50 a minute for the deliberately elongated forty-five-minute call. It cost her $157.50 to cancel the platinum card scam service.

Gwen learned the hard way that there was no quick and easy way to establish credit in America. She realized that she would have to establish credit with a variety of local and national businesses, who over time would help her establish a decent credit profile.

Of course, having an established and readily available credit profile still won't protect you from the myriad of scams out there.

Yo-Yo Auto Loans

In interviewing Nevada attorney general Brian Sandoval and his staff for this book another scheme—the yo-yo auto loan scheme—was identified. Coincidentally, my friend Kristy had been subjected to this "legal" scam only two weeks earlier.

Kristy had always wanted to own a new car. She and her husband, Edwin, had decided the time was right and began shopping around. On a Saturday they found a great deal on an SUV with low 6 percent financing. The car dealer said there would be no problem obtaining the loan. Drive the car home, he said, your credit is fine. Then on Tuesday the dealer called back with bad news. Their credit wasn't good enough to qualify for the 6 percent rate. Instead, the best he could do was a 14 percent rate.

Kristy and Edwin were upset. They had already driven the new car over four hundred miles. The dealer cheerfully informed them they could return the car if they wanted. But did they really want to? Edwin demanded to know how they could sign a contract with credit issues included and then back out of the deal. The dealer pleasantly noted that the contract allowed the dealer to rescind the transaction within fifteen days if the right credit wasn't arranged. As a favor to them, when the 6 percent financing fell through he went and found the 14 percent financing.

For Kristy the ploy was pure manipulation. The car was already hers. It handled well and was fun to drive. The last thing she wanted to do was turn it back in. She and Edwin grudgingly accepted the new higher financing.

Neil Rombardo is a Nevada deputy attorney general in the Carson City office. He deals with yo-yo auto loan schemes. Rombardo explained that the scheme is "legal" since the contract allows the dealer to terminate for a failure to find acceptable credit, and state law does not prohibit such transactions.

Interestingly, while the dealer can terminate within fifteen days under state law, the buyer cannot.

Rombardo noted that while most consumers will reluctantly accept the new financing, a few have been angry enough to take the car back. Tellingly (and not surprisingly) the next day dealers have called these consumers back to say they have miraculously arranged for the original lower financing that was sought. The car was theirs!

To avoid the yo-yo auto loan scam it is advised to line up fixed auto financing with your bank or credit union before you go shopping for a new car. If for some reason you are faced with this scam, Rombardo encourages consumers to report the car dealer to your state's Consumer Affairs Division. Rombardo will be presenting a bill to the next session of the Nevada legislature to outlaw the scheme. Kristy has agreed to testify.

Identity Theft

Just as there are many organized groups—from nationally advertised credit card scamsters to unscrupulous local car dealers—systematically taking advantage of consumers, there are individuals at work trying to steal your very identity and the good credit that comes with it.

Identity theft is a very personal scam. And it can arise from the people close to you.

Jeffrey had a drug problem. He tried not to let anyone around him become aware of it, but he was addicted to cocaine and his close friends and family members all knew it. They couldn't ignore the obvious signs, the hollowed-out cheeks and eyes, the slight twitch in his hands, and the ever constant sniffling.

Jeffrey was a big man used to getting his way. He was the oldest of three brothers and knew how to bully his way forward. He had used cocaine recreationally with friends in college. All had agreed in those days that it was a good social drug, and there were plenty of women attracted to Jeffery because he carried a party night's worth of cocaine. Jeffrey felt alive on cocaine. Always a talker, he had a heightened sense of communicative ability while he was on the drug.

But Jeffrey's friends had moved on. They had all felt the negative effects of the misnamed "good drug." They were seeing the wreckage cocaine inflicted upon their friends. They were seeing lives wasted away.

Jeffrey was in too deep. He couldn't pull back, and found himself in a downward spiral of needing ever more money for his terrible habit and becoming ever less employable for his terrible habit.

No one ever confronted Jeffrey. He was always used to getting his way and talking his way out of any spot. His family was unprepared to deal with such a problem, and could only hope that he would pull out of it. His friends, tired of being hit up for money that was never repaid, started to drift away. Jeffrey was becoming more and more isolated at a time he needed the most help. Only his Uncle Melvin had the fortitude to stand up to him. But Melvin got nowhere.

Jeffery's most recent job was as an insurance claims representative. He could talk to people on the phone. His customers never knew he had a problem. They never saw him in person, and never spoke to him long enough to know the sad truth about Jeffrey.

But Jeffrey's co-workers soon found out.

The claims representative job didn't quite pay Jeffrey enough. He had an expensive cocaine habit that came before rent, food, or any of the other lesser necessities. He needed to make ends meet.

Jeffrey learned that many of the claims reps did personal business on their computers at work. Some did stock trading for their own brokerage accounts while the stock market was open during business hours. A few of the traders were always joking with each other in the break room over their latest hits and misses.

Jeffrey stayed late one day after work. He was in desperate need of money for another few ounces of cocaine. He rationalized that the traders were cheating the company out of work time by doing such personal business. He was justified in his next step. When everyone was gone Jeffrey got onto one of the claims rep's computers. It was easy to get into the brokerage account. It was one click away from their favorites page. The computer was set to remember personal passwords automatically. He worked quickly on the first machine and then rapidly moved to the next cubicle. In less than ten minutes Jeffrey was armed with the sensitive brokerage information for three of his co-workers' accounts. He immediately went home and got to work on his computer. Within an hour Jeffery was able to cash out the brokerage accounts from the comfort of his home. He was flying high once again before any of his co-workers knew what hit them.

Jeffrey liked the ease of this type of fund raising. Like the tens of thousands of other addicts, lowlifes, and assorted black hearts, Jeffrey became an IDBG, an identity theft bad guy, and started looking for other opportunities. On one of the few occasions he was invited to a family function he was parking in front of his Uncle Melvin's modest house as the mail was being delivered. Being the thoughtful nephew, he carried the mail into the house. Then he noticed that Melvin had received a box of new checks in the mail from the bank. Jeffrey sensed a fund-raising opportunity and without anyone noticing threw the box of checks into the trunk of his car.

After the family gathering Jeffrey set about satisfying his habit. Through a friend of his drug dealer he had been introduced to a man who manufactured false identification cards. It was a booming market with all the IDBGs getting into the business. It was extremely easy for Jeffrey to have an ID made featuring Uncle Melvin's information combined with Jeffrey's photo. With the fake ID and the real checks Jeffrey was able to drain Melvin's account by writing checks for cash at a nearby Indian casino. He deserved it, Jeffrey thought in his haze, for always giving him guff about his habit.

The sudden loss of money from his checking account caused Melvin a severe amount of financial strain. He almost lost his house to foreclosure and was assessed with a huge amount of late fees on the multitude of bounced checks. The family was furious. By the handwriting on the checks they knew it was Jeffrey's work.

The family had had enough. Charges were pressed and Jeffrey went to jail. The point to remember here is that identity theft is frequently wrought by people you know. Accordingly, you must be cautious not only with strangers but with acquaintances as well.

Identity theft is now called the fastest growing crime in America. The facts and figures are staggering:

- 27.3 million Americans have been victims of identity theft in the last five years, including 9.91 million people or 4.6 percent of the population in the last year alone.[1]

- Nearly 85 percent of all victims find out about their identity theft case in a negative manner. Only 15 percent of victims find out due to a proactive action taken by a business.[2]

- 16 percent say it was a friend, relative, or co-worker who stole their identity.[3] The true figure may be higher.

- The average time spent by victims dealing with the theft of their identity is about 600 hours, an increase of more than 300 percent over previous studies.[4]

- Last year's identity theft losses to businesses and financial institutions totaled $47.6 billion and consumer victims reported $5 billion in out-of-pocket expenses.[5]

- Because this crime is often misclassified, the thieves have just a 1 in 700 chance of being caught by the federal authorities.[6]

- The emotional impact of identity theft has been found to parallel that of victims of violent crime.[7]

- Roughly half of all adults feel they do not know how to protect themselves against identity theft.[8]

- Children are increasingly becoming victims of identity theft, according to the Identity Theft Resource Center.

---

1. Federal Trade Commission 2003 Identity Theft Survey Report, prepared by Synovate, www.ftc.gov/os/2003/09/synovaterport.pdf.

2. *Identity Theft 2003: The Aftermath.* A study conducted by the Identity Theft Resource Center, www.idtheftcenter.org/idaftermath.pdf.

3. Privacy and American Business 2003 Identity Theft Survey, www.pandab.org/.

4. *Identity Theft 2003.*

5. Federal Trade Commission study.

6. Gartner 2003 survey of 2,445 households, www3.gartner.com/5_about/press_releases/pr21july2003a.jsp.

7. *Identity Theft 2003.*

8. Privacy and American Business survey.

How to Avoid Identity Theft

Given the enormity of the problem it is important for everyone to know how to avoid becoming a victim of identity theft. The following ten tips may keep you from becoming the next statistic.

1. Jealousy guard your Social Security number. This one number can give the wrong person the keys to your castle. Avoid giving it out over the phone. Know that California has a law that prohibits many businesses from requiring your Social Security number. If the national company wants your number tell them they are violating California law (even if you live in Texas). Do not carry your Social Security card with you. Keep it in a safe-deposit box or other secure place.

2. Sign your credit cards as soon as you receive them. It is harder for a criminal to obtain merchandise when your signature is on the card. It is easy for an IDBG to sign your card, get the necessary backup identification, and have a field day with your credit and your identity.

3. Even if you are the most forgetful person on earth do not attach your Social Security number or personal identification number (PIN) to any card you carry with you. In fact, it would be best if you forgot to do that altogether. If you lose that card or it is stolen having those numbers attached will make life easy for an IDBG, and make your life miserable for a while, or even longer.

4. Similarly, don't write your PIN or Social on an invoice or receipt that may be thrown away. You'd be surprised at who is rifling through the trash. Some trashy people.

5. Check your receipts to make sure you received yours and not someone else's information. The someone else may misuse what they just received.

6. Don't give out any confidential information or account numbers to anyone unless you are certain they are worthy of it. And even then think twice about giving it out. As our cases have illustrated, there are many innocent-sounding requests made of you by people last innocent in grade school.

7. Put difficult and unique passwords on your bank accounts, credit cards, and personal accounts. Don't use standard, boring, and easy-to-obtain information like a mother's maiden name or a birth date as a password. Con-

sider instead using cool and obscure Australian place names such as Yarra-wonga, Mullumbimby, or Wagga Wagga. Get out the atlas and have some fun. (If the IDBG after you is an aborigine your luck may have already run out.)

8. If you don't receive your regular statements in the mail contact the creditor immediately. Someone may be stealing your mail. As well, if your mail is not dropped through a slot into your house but rather left outside in an exposed mailbox you may want to reconsider where you receive your mail. An option is to have creditor statements and confidential mailings directed to a secure mail-receiving service.

9. Check your credit report on a regular basis for signs of improper account activity, new and unknown account openings, and other warning signs. Be proactive in protecting your credit and your identity.

10. Buy a shredder.

What to Do if You're a Victim of Identity Theft

By taking these steps you will reduce your chances of becoming the next identity theft victim. Nevertheless, for all your proactive steps, it still may happen and you need to know what to do.

The Federal Trade Commission has become actively involved in the problems of identity theft. The FTC suggests promptly taking the following four steps:

1. Notify the fraud departments at Experian, TransUnion, and Equifax that you are an identity theft victim. Request that a "fraud alert" be placed in your file. Prepare a victim's statement requesting that creditors call you before changing current accounts or opening new ones. Begin frequently reviewing updated copies of your credit reports to ensure that no additional fraudulent accounts are opened.

2. Call all your creditors, including utilities, the phone company, credit card companies, and the like, and ask to speak to a representative in the fraud (or security) department. Find out if any existing accounts have been tampered with or if any new accounts have been improperly opened. Close any account that has been tampered with and then open a new account. As

suggested, use unique, difficult-to-guess passwords such as obscure cities in Australia or elsewhere around the globe.

3. File a police report in your home town and, if applicable, in the city where the identity theft occurred. While we all know how useful filing a police report can be ("Oh, I see this isn't a drug case. We'll get back to you."), in one civil case out of a thousand the local authorities actually do something. You might be the lucky one. (Under new FACTA rules you'll have to file a report anyway.)

4. Fill out an identity theft fraud affidavit, which is available online at www.consumer.gov/idtheft. This can save you time by giving you one form to fill out, and will be required by many creditors.

As mentioned, the FTC is very interested in this large and growing problem. They maintain a special Identity Theft Hotline at 1-877-IDTHEFT (1-877-438-4338). You can also file a complaint online at the following Web site: www.consumer.gov/idtheft.

Chapter XIV

Winning with Credit

We've given you a lot of information about how the credit system works. Now it's time to put it all together. There are several basic principles to using good debt to your advantage. Learning these are a critical part of becoming financially independent.

Using Good Debt

#1: Have a Positive Goal. Getting out of debt by and large is a negative goal. It implies you don't want something: debt. But building wealth is a positive goal. That's much more motivating. So while you are creating your plan to get out of debt, at the same time figure out how that will free up cash flow for you to devote to your positive wealth-building goals. Keep your eye on the real prize.

#2: Live Rich, Even if You Aren't. Robert's rich dad never said he should be cheap to reach his goals. In fact, he told Robert that he didn't understand people who were too cheap. "You can become rich by being cheap. But the problem is, even though you're rich, you're still cheap." Instead he advised

Robert to find out what he wanted, learn the price, and then decide if he wanted to pay the price.

Getting out of debt will teach you a lot about yourself. When your ultimate goal, creating wealth, becomes more important than the stuff you're wasting money on, you'll find the way.

Read books on becoming wealthy. Start a mastermind group. Immerse yourself in thoughts about what you're working toward so you can stop focusing on the negatives of your current situation. Learning from people wealthier than you will help you set your sights much higher than you have already.

#3: Know When to Cut Your Losses. Bad things happen to good people. Responsible, caring people get sick, lose their jobs, get divorced, and even file for bankruptcy. At some point you have to decide to cut your losses and start moving forward. It's tragic to see people wiping out what little wealth they've squirreled away in their retirement funds in a last-ditch to pay their credit card bill or save their credit rating. It's terrible to see people lose their homes to foreclosure because they aren't willing to face the reality of their situation.

Many of the top financial successes in this country have been through personal failure, including bankruptcy. They went on to create personal fortunes and contribute to worthy causes. Whether it's filing for bankruptcy, entering a debt negotiation program, or selling your home through a short sale to avoid foreclosure, if you're in a crisis, do what you need to do and then start moving forward again.

#4: Get Smart About Credit. Start reading the fine print on your credit card statements and cardholder agreements. Get savvy about shopping for lower rates. Find explanations for terms you don't understand. The money you save can be used to make you many more dollars in the future!

#5: Know the Difference Between Good Debt and Bad Debt. Good debt helps you leverage your financial life to create wealth-producing assets. Bad debt sucks your money away because you end up spending much more for the things you buy, many of which are gone by the time you pay the bill. Before you take on new debt, ask yourself whether it is good debt or bad debt.

Business Credit

When you are building wealth, you will no doubt at some point create a business, whether it's a small home-based network marketing business or a company that grows to the size where it goes public. The proper use of credit can be an important factor in successfully advancing your prospects.

Business credit can create many advantages. It can shield you from personal liability if things don't pan out, and more importantly, it can allow you to leverage small amounts of money to create large amounts of wealth. (See the Resources section for more advice on building a business credit profile.)

The strategic use of debt in business can easily become complex and convoluted. Without going into a great deal of detail there are some important points to consider when using debt to advance your business interests.

Debt comes in a variety of flavors. Borrowings from a bank and financings from suppliers and other vendors are pure vanilla and quite common. Unfunded pension liabilities and off-balance sheet items (such as in the Enron scandal) are more exotic, and, lately, more bitter.

Whether you are establishing a first-time credit line for your business or are buying a business with existing debt in place, there are crucial provisions found in all loan agreements that you may not be aware of—but need to know for your benefit.

The initial items to review and consider are, as one would expect, the most basic. Whether you review the terms with your attorney and/or CPA, or solely on your own, you are going to want to have a clear understanding of the following:

1. The amount of the loan. It may sound obvious but some loans can be revolving (or variable) lines of credit that have various limits. Be sure to understand how much you are borrowing. Know your limits.

2. The type of debt. Is the loan based on a line of credit, a promissory note, or a mortgage against property? The type of debt will affect many of the other issues considered below.

3. The interest rate and repayment terms. Does the interest rate fluctuate or is it fixed? How is the interest rate calculated? Is there a balloon payment, meaning that all of the principal and interest is due at a fixed future

date (e.g., five years), or is the loan fully amortized over a longer period, such as thirty years? Is there a penalty for prepayment?

4. The security and priority of the debt. Is the debt secured by company assets and property? Or is it unsecured, meaning that no collateral for repayment has been provided? Which debt has priority over any other borrowings? Be sure to discuss security and priority issues with your advisors.

5. The personal guarantees involved. Do you need to personally guarantee the lender that you will make good on the loan if the company does not? You will want to carefully consider signing a personal guarantee. Then again, you may find it is the only way you are going to get certain types of loans.

6. Reporting obligations. Some loans will require that you report back to the lender on your status, and provide tax returns and financial statements on an ongoing basis. Failure to report back can result in the loan being called. Know what you must report.

7. Events of default. Like the failure to report, the loan agreement may contain one or more default items, which if not complied with can result in the loan being called. Know what you need to do when.

8. Affirmative and negative covenants. These types of agreements in loan documents are subtle and rarely comprehended, yet very important. They are deserving of a greater discussion.

An affirmative covenant is an agreement by the borrower to follow certain rules and guidelines laid down by the lender. Conversely, a negative covenant is an agreement by the borrower that it will not engage in certain activities or allow certain conditions to exist.

An example of an affirmative covenant would be a requirement in the loan document that the company file all of its tax returns and other government filings on time. That's innocent enough. You need to do it anyway. Another affirmative covenant may require the company to provide the lender with all such filings as well.

The area of concern generally surrounds negative covenants. Frequently, loans will feature "financial maintenance" covenants, which restrict the company's activities. The lender, naturally, doesn't want its money put at risk by any imprudent steps taken by the company. Accordingly, negative covenants will be inserted to prevent future borrowings, to limit capital expenditures and company acquisitions, and even to limit bonuses and dividends to company owners.

Negative covenants can be so broad and far-reaching as to stop the company in its tracks. If your company is in a high growth mode you are going to want to carefully consider entering into a loan with negative covenants that prevent your growth. Even if you have a stable, cash-flowing business such as a car wash you are going to want to avoid a loan that limits distributions to the owners.

Be sure to understand the meanings and consequences of affirmative and negative covenants. If they are not suitable for you and your company, negotiate to have them removed. Or go elsewhere for a loan. Lenders quietly respect the borrower who is ready and willing to look elsewhere.

Credit is an important money tool for business success. Just be certain that you and, hopefully, your team of advisors understand all of the terms and conditions of the agreements you enter into. Never be afraid to walk away from any type of loan that seems too onerous. If it seems unfair at the start it's not going to get any better later.

Shop around, find the right lenders to work with, and use credit to your advantage.

Conclusion

You Can Get Out of Debt

As we have learned throughout this book, you can get out of debt and win with credit. Millions of Americans have done it before you, and hopefully you will be one of the many millions who will do so in the future.

With a positive goal, a clear idea of the difference between good debt and bad debt, and by taking advantage of the resources in the following section you too can win.

Good Luck.

Appendix A

Sample Credit Report

experian

Prepared for
JOHN Q CONSUMER

Report number
1234567890

Report date
January 2, 2004

experian.com/disputes

Page 1 of 7

Personal Credit Report

About this report

Experian collects and organizes information about you and your credit history from public records, your creditors and other reliable sources. We make your credit history available to your current and prospective creditors and employers as allowed by law. We do not grant credit or evaluate credit history. Personal data about you may be made available to companies whose products and services may interest you.

Important decisions about creditworthiness are based on the information in this report. Before contacting us, you should review it carefully for accuracy.

Information affecting your creditworthiness

Below is a summary of the information contained in this report

Potentially negative items listed

Public records	2
Accounts with creditors and others	5
Accounts in good standing	3

If you believe that information is inaccurate, use our new, easy-to-use online dispute service at www.experian.com/yourcredit.

If you have questions
Locate your Report Number, then, contact us.

For efficient, self-directed service, log on to **www.experian.com/disputes** and select **"Dispute it online"**.

For assistance, call
800-XXX-XXXX
M - F 9am - 5pm in your time zone.

Information is updated frequently, so you should **contact us within 90 days** from the date on this report.

To order a copy of your Experian Credit Score Report, call 1 888 322 5583.

Protect and manage your credit with Credit Manager
www.creditexpert.com/protect

To submit your request for investigation in writing, include your full name, current mailing address, Social Security number, date of birth, your Report Number, the account number of the item you are disputing, and the <u>specific</u> reason why you believe the information is inaccurate. Send all of the requested information to P.O. Box 9595, Allen, TX 75013.

experian

Prepared for
JOHN Q CONSUMER
Report number
1234567890

Report date
January 2, 2004
www.experian.com/disputes
Call 1 800 XXX XXXX

Page 2 of 7

Information affecting your creditworthiness

Items listed with dashes before and after the number, *for example -- 1 --*, may have a potentially negative effect on your future credit extension and are listed first on the report.

Credit grantors may carefully review the items listed below when they check your credit history. Please note that the account information connected with some public records, such as bankruptcy, also may appear with your credit accounts listed later in this report.

Your statement(s)

At your request, we've included the following statement every time your credit report is requested.

"My identification has been used without my consent on applications for credit. Please call me at 999 999 9999 before approving credit in my name."

Public Records

Source/ Identification number	Location number	Date filed/ Date resolved	Responsibility	Claim amount/ Liability amount	Status details
-- 1 -- **HOLLY CO DIST CT** 305 MAIN STREET HOLLY NJ 08060	B312P7659	3-1997 / NA	Joint	$3,756 / NA	Status: civil claim judgment filed. Plaintiff: Dime Savings. This item is scheduled to continue on record until 3-2004. This item was verified on 8-1997 and remained unchanged.
-- 2 -- **BROWN TOWN HALL** 10 COURT ST BROWN, NJ 02809	BK443PG14	11-1997/ 10-1998	Joint	$57,786 / NA	Status: chapter 7 bankruptcy discharged. This item is scheduled to continue on record until 11-2007. This item was verified on 8-1997 and remained unchanged.

experian

Prepared for
JOHN Q CONSUMER

Report number
1234567890

Report date
January 2, 2004
www.experian.com/disputes
Call 1 800 XXX XXXX

Page 3 of 7

Credit items

Source/ Account number (except last few digits)	Date opened/ Reported since	Date of status/ Last reported	Type/ Terms/ Monthly payment	Responsibility	Credit limit or original amount/ High balance	Recent balance/ Recent payment	Status details
- 3 -- FIDELITY BK NA 300 FIDELITY PLAZA NORTHSHORE NJ 08902 46576000024....	6-1994/ 6-1994	12-1996/ 12-1996	Installment 10 Months/ $0	Individual	$4,549/ NA	$4,549 as of 12-1996/	Status: charge off. $4,549 written off in 12-1996. This account is scheuled to continue on record until 12-2003
- 4 -- B.B. CREDIT 35 WASHINGTON ST DEDHAM MA 547631236	10-1990/ 4-1995	3-2002/ 3-2002	Installment/ 80 months/ $34	Individual	$8,500/ $8,500	$0 as of 3-2000/ $34	Status: Debt re-included in chapter 7 bankruptcy. $389 written off in 3-2002 Account history: Collection as of 9-2000 thru 6-2001 90 days as of 7-2000 60 days as of 11-1999, 6-2000 30 days as of 9-1999, 1-2000 and 2 other times. This account is scheduled to continue on record until 6-2007. This item was verified and updated on 6- 2001.

Original creditor: Bally's Health Club/Personal Services.

experian

Prepared for
JOHN Q CONSUMER
Report number
1234567890

Report date
January 2, 2004
www.experian.com/disputes
Call 1 800 XXX XXXX

Page 4 of 7

Credit items

Source/ Account number (except last few digits)	Date opened/ Reported since	Date of status/ Last reported	Type/ Terms/ Monthly payment	Responsibility	Credit limit or original amount/ High balance	Recent balance/ Recent payment	Status details
5 **FIRST CREDIT UNION** 78 WASHINGTON LN LANEVILLE TX 76362 129474	3-1996/ 3-1996	11-1998/ 11-1998	Installment/ 48 Months/ $420		$17,856/ NA	$0 as of 11-1998/ $420	Status: open/never late.
6 **AMERICA FINANCE CORP** PO BOX 8633 COLLEY IL 60126 6376001172....	6-1993/ 7-1993	11-1998/ 11-1998	Revolving/ NA / $400		$0/ $18,251	$0 as of 11-1998/	Status: card reported lost or stolen. This account is scheduled to continue on record until 11-2008.
7 **NATIONAL CREDIT CARD** 100 THE PLAZA LANEVILLE NJ 08905	6-1993/ 6-1993	6-2003/ 6-2003	Revolving/ NA / $0	Joint with JANE CONSUMER	$8,000/ $8,569	$0 as of 11-1998/	Status: open/never late.

Purchased from CITIBANK VISA

experian

Prepared for
JOHN Q CONSUMER
Report number
1234567890

Report date
January 2, 2004
www.experian.com/disputes
Call 1 800 XXX XXXX

Page 5 of 7

Your use of credit

The information listed below provides additional detail about your accounts, showing up to 24 months of balance history and your credit limit, high balance or original loan amount. Not all balance history is reported to Experian, so some of your accounts may not appear. Also, some credit grantors may not update the information more than once in the same month.

Source/Account number

Date opened/ Reported since

6 AMERICA FINANCE CO CORP
6376001172...

11-1998/$0	10-1998/$4,329	8-1998/$0	5-1998/$0	2-1998/$250	1-1998/$0	12-1997/$2,951
9-1997/$3,451	7-1997/$4,251	5-1997/$4,561			

Between 1-1994 and 11-1998 your credit limit was unknown.

7 National CREDIT CARD
420000638...

4-2003/$0	2-2003/$225	11-2002/$425	9-2002/$542	7-2002/$300	6-2002/$686	4-2002/$1,400
3-2002/$2,500	1-2002/$2,774	12-2001/$599	9-2001/$873	7-2001/$1,413	5-2001/$1,765
4-2001/$2,387	3-2001/$3,400	2-2001/$3,212	1-2001/$4,412	

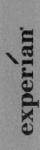

Prepared for
JOHN Q CONSUMER

Report number
1234567890

Report date
January 2, 2004
www.experian.com/disputes
Call 1 800 XXX XXXX

Page 6 of 7

Others who have requested your credit history

Listed below are all those who have received information from us in the recent past about your credit history.

Requests initiated by you

You took actions, such as completing a credit application, that allowed the following sources to review your information. Please note that the following information is part of your credit history and is included in our reports to others.

Source	Date	Comments
ABC MORTGAGE 64 MAPLE ROSEVILLE MD 02849	10-18-2002	Real estate loan of $214,000 on behalf of State Bank with 30 year repayment terms. This inquiry is scheduled to continue on record until 10-2004

Requests viewed only by you

You may not have initiated the following requests for your credit history, so you may not recognize each source. We offer credit information about you to those with a permissible purpose, for example to:

- other creditors who want to offer you preapproved credit;
- an employer who wishes to extend an offer of employment;
- a potential investor in assessing the risk of a current obligation;
- Experian Consumer Assistance to process a report for you;
- your current creditors to monitor your accounts (date listed may reflect only the most recent request).

We report these requests **only** to you as a record of activities, and we do not include **any** of these requests on credit reports to others.

Source	Date
Experian PO BOX 2002 ALLEN TX 75013	3-03
WORLD BANK 4578 DRIVE NORTH YORKVILLE NY 03939	3-03, 12-02, 9-02, 6-02, 3-02, 12-01, 9-01, 7-01
FIDELITY BANK NA 300 FIDELITY PLAZA NORTHSHORE NJ 08902	1-03, 7-02, 1-02, 7-01
NATIONAL CREDIT CARD 100 THE PLAZA LANEVILLE NJ 08905	7-02, 2-02

Prepared for
JOHN Q CONSUMER

Report number
1234567890

Report date
January 2, 2004
www.experian.com/disputes
Call 1 800 XXX XXXX

Page 7 of 7

experian

Personal information
The following information is reported to us **by you, your creditors**
and **other sources.** Each source may report your personal
information differently, which may result in variations of your name,
address, Social Security number, etc. As part of our fraud -prevention
program, a notice with additional information may appear.

Names
JOHN Q CONSUMER

Residences
Our records show you currently are a homeowner. The geographical code shown
with each address identifies the state, county, census tract, block group and
Metropolitan Statistical Area associated with each address.

Address	Type of address	Geographical code
7972 PADDOCK CT LANEVILLE TX 71144-1735	Single family	0-192053-3-0
1704 BEVERLY AVE SPRING LAKE NJ 07762-2004	Single family	0-224681-25-0
2562 GARDEN DR BRIDGE NJ 00160-9712	Single family	0-9004-93-0

Social Security number variations
228-00-0117
282-00-0117
228-00-1017

Date of birth
10-05-1966

Driver's license number
TX 9840295

Telephone numbers
XXX XXX XXXX

Spouse's Name
JANE

Notices
The first Social Security number listed shows that credit was established before the
number was issued.

000001234   F-000-00000-1503002

Appendix B

Sample Letters

Sample Letter to Collection Agency Requesting Verification of Debt

Your name and address

Date

Name and address of collection agency

RE: Account number (list account number if given)

Dear Sir or Madam,

I was recently informed that I owe a debt in the amount of $ (list amount of debt) to (list original creditor).

I don't believe that debt is correct. Please send me written verification of the debt.

Sincerely,

Your name

Sample Letter to Collection Agency Requesting Them to Stop Contacting You

Your name and address

Date

Name and address of collection agency

RE: Account number (list account number if given)

Dear Sir or Madam,

I have been in contact with your agency about a debt in the amount of $ (list amount of debt) to (list original creditor).

I ask you to stop contacting me about that debt. (You may choose to give a reason: As I have stated I don't believe I owe it, I cannot pay any portion of the debt at this time, or whatever is appropriate).

Thank you,

Your name

Sample Letter to Collection Agency
For Settlement of Debt

Your name and address

Date

Name and address of collection agency

RE: Account number (list account number if given)

Dear Sir or Madam,

I have been in contact with your agency about a debt in the amount of $ (list amount of debt) to (list original creditor).

Today we agreed that if I pay $ (amount of settled debt) that this debt will be settled in full. You will promptly notify the creditor that there is no balance due on the debt. You will also promptly notify the credit bureaus (either that the debt has been settled with no balance due, or that it will be removed from the credit bureau records).

When I receive your written confirmation of these terms of our agreement, I will make the payment we agreed upon.

Sincerely,

Your name

Sample Letter to Collection Agency For Payment Arrangement

Your name and address

Date

Name and address of collection agency

RE: Account number (list account number if given)

Dear (name of collector you've been dealing with),

I have been in contact with your agency about a debt in the amount of $ (list amount of debt) to (list original creditor).

As we have discussed, I am making every effort to pay this debt as quickly as I can given my current financial situation.

We have agreed that I will pay $ (dollar amount) on a $ (monthly, weekly, or other) basis. I have included the first check based on our agreement to-day. If this is not our agreement, please return the enclosed check and contact me to discuss other arrangements.

Thank you,

Your name

Sample Letter to Credit Reporting Agency Disputing Wrong Information

Note: Handwrite your dispute if your handwriting is legible

Your name and address
Your Social Security number
Your credit report number

Date

Name and address of credit reporting agency

Dear Sir or Madam,

I am disputing the following account listed on my credit report:

(List account details)

It (choose one of the following or modify for your needs: is not my account, is too old to legally be reported, has an incorrect balance, was never late, has been paid in full, and so forth).

Please investigate and reply as soon as possible.

Thank you,

Your name

Sample Letter to Lender or Furnisher Disputing Wrong Information

Note: Handwrite your dispute if your handwriting is legible.

Your name and address
Your Social Security number
Your account number (if available)

Date

Name and address of lender or furnisher

Dear Sir or Madam,

I am disputing the following account listed on my (Experian, Equifax, and/or TransUnion) credit report:

(List account details)

It (choose one of the following or modify for your needs: is not my account, is too old to legally be reported, has an incorrect balance, was never late, has been paid in full, and so forth).

Please investigate and reply as soon as possible.

Thank you,

Your name

Appendix C

Key Credit Protection Laws

THE FAIR DEBT COLLECTION PRACTICES ACT
Highlights

This is a summary of some of the important provisions of the FDCPA. To read the complete Act, visit the SuccessDNA.com Credit Center.

§ 802. Congressional findings and declarations of purpose
[15 USC 1692]
(a) There is abundant evidence of the use of abusive, deceptive, and unfair debt collection practices by many debt collectors. Abusive debt collection practices contribute to the number of personal bankruptcies, to marital instability, to the loss of jobs, and to invasions of individual privacy.

§ 805. Communication in connection with debt collection
[15 USC 1692c]
(a) COMMUNICATION WITH THE CONSUMER GENERALLY. Without the prior consent of the consumer given directly to the debt collector or the express permission of a court of competent jurisdiction, a debt collector may not communicate with a consumer in connection with the collection of any debt—

(1) at any unusual time or place or a time or place known or which should be known to be inconvenient to the consumer. In the absence of knowledge of circumstances to the contrary, a debt collector shall assume that the convenient time for communicating with a consumer is after 8 o'clock antimeridian and before 9 o'clock postmeridian, local time at the consumer's location;

(3) at the consumer's place of employment if the debt collector knows or has reason to know that the consumer's employer prohibits the consumer from receiving such communication.

(b) COMMUNICATION WITH THIRD PARTIES. Except as provided in section 804, without the prior consent of the consumer given directly to the debt collector, or the express permission of a court of competent jurisdiction, or as reasonably necessary to effectuate a post judgment judicial remedy, a debt collector may not communicate, in connection with the collection of any debt, with any person other than a consumer, his attorney, a consumer reporting agency if otherwise permitted by law, the creditor, the attorney of the creditor, or the attorney of the debt collector.

(c) CEASING COMMUNICATION. If a consumer notifies a debt collector in writing that the consumer refuses to pay a debt or that the consumer wishes the debt collector to cease further communication with the consumer, the debt collector shall not communicate further with the consumer with respect to such debt, except . . .

> (3) where applicable, to notify the consumer that the debt collector or creditor intends to invoke a specified remedy.

(d) For the purpose of this section, the term "consumer" includes the consumer's spouse, parent (if the consumer is a minor), guardian, executor, or administrator.

§ 806. Harassment or abuse [15 USC 1692d]
A debt collector may not engage in any conduct the natural consequence of which is to harass, oppress, or abuse any person in connection with the collection of a debt. Without limiting the general application of the foregoing, the following conduct is a violation of this section:

> (1) The use or threat of use of violence or other criminal means to harm the physical person, reputation, or property of any person.

> (2) The use of obscene or profane language or language the natural consequence of which is to abuse the hearer or reader.

> (5) Causing a telephone to ring or engaging any person in telephone conversation repeatedly or continuously with intent to annoy, abuse, or harass any person at the called number.

> (6) Except as provided in section 804, the placement of telephone calls without meaningful disclosure of the caller's identity.

§ 807. False or misleading representations [15 USC 1692e]
A debt collector may not use any false, deceptive, or misleading representation or means in connection with the collection of any debt. Without

limiting the general application of the foregoing, the following conduct is a violation of this section:

(1) The false representation or implication that the debt collector is vouched for, bonded by, or affiliated with the United States or any State, including the use of any badge, uniform, or facsimile thereof.

(2) The false representation of—

(A) the character, amount, or legal status of any debt; or

(B) any services rendered or compensation which may be lawfully received by any debt collector for the collection of a debt.

(3) The false representation or implication that any individual is an attorney or that any communication is from an attorney.

(4) The representation or implication that nonpayment of any debt will result in the arrest or imprisonment of any person or the seizure, garnishment, attachment, or sale of any property or wages of any person unless such action is lawful and the debt collector or creditor intends to take such action.

(5) The threat to take any action that cannot legally be taken or that is not intended to be taken.

(7) The false representation or implication that the consumer committed any crime or other conduct in order to disgrace the consumer.

(8) Communicating or threatening to communicate to any person credit information which is known or which should be known to be false, including the failure to communicate that a disputed debt is disputed.

(9) The use or distribution of any written communication which simulates or is falsely represented to be a document authorized, issued, or approved by any court, official, or agency of the United States or any State, or which creates a false impression as to its source, authorization, or approval.

(10) The use of any false representation or deceptive means to collect or attempt to collect any debt or to obtain information concerning a consumer.

§ 808. Unfair practices [15 USC 1692f]

A debt collector may not use unfair or unconscionable means to collect or attempt to collect any debt. Without limiting the general application of the foregoing, the following conduct is a violation of this section:

(1) The collection of any amount (including any interest, fee, charge, or expense incidental to the principal obligation) unless such amount is expressly authorized by the agreement creating the debt or permitted by law.

(2) The acceptance by a debt collector from any person of a check or other payment instrument postdated by more than five days unless such person is notified in writing of the debt collector's intent to deposit such check or instrument not more than ten nor less than three business days prior to such deposit.

(3) The solicitation by a debt collector of any postdated check or other postdated payment instrument for the purpose of threatening or instituting criminal prosecution.

(4) Depositing or threatening to deposit any postdated check or other postdated payment instrument prior to the date on such check or instrument.

(6) Taking or threatening to take any nonjudicial action to effect dispossession or disablement of property if—

(A) there is no present right to possession of the property claimed as collateral through an enforceable security interest;

(B) there is no present intention to take possession of the property; or

(C) the property is exempt by law from such dispossession or disablement.

§ 809. Validation of debts [15 USC 1692g]

(a) Within five days after the initial communication with a consumer in connection with the collection of any debt, a debt collector shall, unless the following information is contained in the initial communication or the consumer has paid the debt, send the consumer a written notice containing—

(1) the amount of the debt;

(2) the name of the creditor to whom the debt is owed;

(3) a statement that unless the consumer, within thirty days after receipt of the notice, disputes the validity of the debt, or any portion thereof, the debt will be assumed to be valid by the debt collector;

(4) a statement that if the consumer notifies the debt collector in writing within the thirty-day period that the debt, or any portion thereof, is disputed, the debt collector will obtain verification of the debt or a copy of a judgment against the consumer and a copy of such verification or judgment will be mailed to the consumer by the debt collector; and

(5) a statement that, upon the consumer's written request within the thirty-day period, the debt collector will provide the consumer with the name and address of the original creditor, if different from the current creditor.

(b) If the consumer notifies the debt collector in writing within the thirty-day period described in subsection (a) that the debt, or any portion thereof, is disputed, or that the consumer requests the name and address of the original creditor, the debt collector shall cease collection of the debt, or any disputed portion thereof, until the debt collector obtains verification of the debt or any copy of a judgment, or the name and address of the original creditor, and a copy of such verification or judgment, or name and address of the original creditor, is mailed to the consumer by the debt collector.

§ 811. Legal actions by debt collectors [15 USC 1692i]

(a) Any debt collector who brings any legal action on a debt against any consumer shall—

(1) in the case of an action to enforce an interest in real property securing the consumer's obligation, bring such action only in a judicial district or similar legal entity in which such real property is located; or

(2) in the case of an action not described in paragraph (1), bring such action only in the judicial district or similar legal entity—

(A) in which such consumer signed the contract sued upon; or

(B) in which such consumer resides at the commencement of the action.

(b) Nothing in this title shall be construed to authorize the bringing of legal actions by debt collectors.

Appendix D

Worksheets

Worksheet for Tracking Spending

Spending Item	Amount Budgeted	Actual
Monthly Income		
Source:		
Source:		
Source:		
Total Income:		
Taxes		
Federal		
State		
Personal property		
Other:		
Total Taxes:		
Housing		
Mortgage or rent		
Property taxes		
Homeowner's/Renter's insurance		
Electric		
Gas or oil		

Spending Item	Amount Budgeted	Actual
Water		
Trash collection		
Other utilities		
Association/Condo fees		
Landscaping		
Cleaning		
Maintenance/Repairs		
Alarm system		
Telephone—local service		
Telephone—long distance		
Cell phone		
Other:		
Other:		
Total Housing:		
Automobile (boat, or motorcycle)		
Payment auto 1		
Gas auto 1		
Maintenance auto 1		
Repair auto 1		
Payment auto 2		
Gas auto 2		
Maintenance auto 2		
Repair auto 2		
Payment auto 3		
Gas auto 3		
Maintenance 3		
Repair auto 3		
Parking		

Spending Item	Amount Budgeted	Actual
Public transportation		
Other		
Other		
Total Auto		
Food		
Groceries		
Lunch/Meals at work		
Snacks		
Kids' lunches		
Pizza delivery/carryout		
Fast food		
Meals out		
Coffee/Beverages		
Other:		
Other:		
Total Food		
Education		
Tuition		
Books		
Supplies		
Other:		
Other:		
Total Education		
Health		
Doctor visits/copays		
Wellness services		

Spending Item	Amount Budgeted	Actual
Prescription medicine		
Over-the-counter medicine		
Dentist		
Vision (including glasses/contacts)		
Supplements		
Other:		
Total Health		
Entertainment		
Movies/Concerts		
Movie rentals		
Cable TV		
Internet service		
Sporting events		
Books		
Magazine subscriptions		
CDs/Music		
Birthday parties		
Holiday parties		
Other:		
Other:		
Total Entertainment		
Insurance		
Disability		
Life		
Credit		
Auto		
Health		

Spending Item	*Amount Budgeted*	*Actual*
Private mortgage insurance		
Umbrella policy		
Boat insurance		
Extended warranty		
Other:		
Total Insurance		
Pets		
Food		
Medical		
Supplies		
Grooming		
Other:		
Total Pets		
Clothing		
Professional attire		
Leisure attire		
Hosiery/Socks		
Underwear/Lingerie		
Shoes/Accessories		
Jewelry		
Dry cleaning/Alterations		
Total Clothing		
Personal Care		
Haircuts/Perms/Coloring		
Manicure/Pedicure/Waxing		
Gym membership/Exercise classes		

Spending Item	Amount Budgeted	Actual
Makeup		
Toiletries		
Other:		
Other:		
Total Personal Care		
Child Care		
Day-care/Tuition		
Extracurricular		
Baby-sitting		
Toys		
Gifts		
Summer camp		
Clothing		
Allowance		
Other:		
Other:		
Total Child Care		
Vacation		
Airfare/Gas		
Lodging		
Food		
Souvenirs		
Gifts		
Other:		
Other:		
Total Vacation		

Spending Item	Amount Budgeted	Actual
Holidays		
Gifts		
Decorating		
Entertainment		
Other:		
Other:		
Total Holidays		
Charitable		
Church/Synagogue/House of worship		
Other:		
Other:		
Other:		
Total Charitable		
Miscellaneous		
Cigarettes		
Hobby		
Other:		
Other:		
Other:		
Other:		
Total Miscellaneous		

Source: Ultimate Credit Solutions Inc. Reprinted with permission.

Debt Worksheet

Creditor	Good or Bad Debt?	APR%	New APR	Balance	Minimum Payment

Total Monthly Debt Payment: _____

How to Use This Worksheet

Make a copy of this chart, since you will have to update it periodically.

Creditor: List each creditor in the first column.

Good Debt or Bad Debt? Write "Good" next to the debt that is good debt, "Bad" next to the debt that is bad debt. Paying off bad debt is your priority.

APR: Next list the interest rate. If your credit card has balances with different interest rates, an effective interest rate should be listed. Use that here.

New APR: When you call to negotiate a lower interest rate, note the rate the issuer will give you here. If you can't successfully negotiate, simply use a check mark so you at least know you've tried. Try again once you pay some balances down.

Balance: List your current balance. On bad debts, stop charging!

Minimum Payment: List the required minimum payment here.

Once you have completed this list, decide which debt elimination strategy you prefer to use: 1) eliminating the high-interest bad debt first to save the most in interest payments over the life of these debts; or 2) Robert and Kim Kiyosaki's method of first paying off the debt with the lowest total balance to quickly give yourself success in your debt elimination plan (see Chapter 4). Now highlight the target debt you'll be paying off first. When you have paid that one off, target the next debt on your list and pay that one off, and so on until you become debt-free. Now start building wealth!

Appendix E

Resources

Resources for Success
The SuccessDNA Web site offers numerous resources to help implement the advice given in this book. Visit www.successdna.com.

Better Business Bureau
To check out a company, visit www.bbb.org. If the company is not listed in the national database, you will be referred to a local Better Business Bureau that can help.

Build Business Credit and Business Credit Profile
Learn how to establish a strong business credit history and credit profile and build a winning strategy for your business's financing needs at www.successdna.com.

Counseling

Credit Counseling Service: For a referral to a credit counseling agency, visit the SuccessDNA Web site at www.successdna.com.

Debtors Anonymous: Operated under the same principles as Alcoholics Anonymous, DA helps chronic debtors stop getting into debt. To find if there is a group in your area, or for more information, write: Debtors Anonymous, General Service Office, PO Box 920888, Needham, MA 02492-0009. Phone: 781-453-2743; Fax: 781-453-2745; www.debtors anonymous.org.

Cooperative Extension Service: You can often find excellent money management counseling, seminars, or publications from your local cooperative extension service. To find a local office, look under the local government listings in your phone book or visit www.reeusda.gov.

Debt Negotiation and Settlement: For a referral to a debt negotiation and settlement firm, visit the SuccessDNA Web site at www.successdna.com.

Financial Recovery Institute: Financial Recovery counseling is a structured process that helps clients transform their relationship with money. It seeks to treat the whole person, including addressing the client's history with, and emotions relating to, money. Visit www.financialrecovery.com or call 877-913-9677.

Housing Help: For a referral to a company that can help you work out problems paying your mortgage, visit www.successdna.com.

Computer/Internet Programs

Visit the SuccessDNA.com Web site for more information on these three programs:

Everyday Wealth: An affordable monthly online service that includes monthly credit report, rapid repayment plan, identity theft insurance, and much more.

Mvelopes Personal: Great software for managing your finances, budgeting, and bill paying.

Debt Blaster: An easy-to-use software program that shows you how to get out of debt in the fastest way possible, with charts and graphs, payoff scenarios you can change, and much more.

Credit Bureaus

You can order a copy of your credit report by contacting the three major credit agencies listed below. *Free annual copies* will become available from late 2004 through late 2005. Check SuccessDNA.com for updated info.

Equifax
Atlanta GA
1-800-685-1111
www.equifax.com

Experian (formerly TRW)
Allen TX
1-888-397-3742
www.experian.com

TransUnion Consumer Relations
Chester PA
1-800-888-4213
www.transunion.com

When you request your credit report, include your full name (including maiden name or generation, such as junior or senior, I or II), your spouse's name, Social Security number, year of birth, your complete addresses for the past five years including zip codes. Sign and date your request and include some proof of your current address, such as a copy of your driver's license or a recent billing statement. If you have been turned down for credit recently, include a copy of your denial letter.

State Limits on Credit Report Prices

California: $8 per copy
Colorado: one free copy annually
Connecticut: $5.00 for the first copy annually
Georgia: two free copies annually
Maine: $2.00 plus photocopying charges
Maryland: one free copy annually, then $5.25
Massachusetts: one free copy annually
Minnesota: $3.00 per copy
New Jersey: one free copy annually
Vermont: one free copy annually, then $7.50
Virgin Islands: $1 per copy

Debt Collectors
ACA International—The Association of Credit and Collection Professionals is the trade association for debt collectors. Visit www.collector.com or write: ACA, PO Box 39106, Minneapolis, MN 55439-0106; Phone: 952-926-6547.

Stop Debt Collectors Cold! is an e-book written by consumer law attorney John Ventura. Visit SuccessDNA.com for more information.

Government Agencies
Comptroller of the Currency: Handles complaints about national banks (banks with the words "National" or "NA" in their name). Visit www.occ.treas.gov or call 800-613-6743.

Federal Deposit Insurance Corporation (FDIC): Handles complaints about FDIC-insured state banks that are not members of the Federal Reserve System.

Federal Reserve System: The Board of Governors of the Federal Reserve System handles complaints about state-chartered banks and trust companies that are members of the Federal Reserve System.

Federal Trade Commission: Contact the FTC at www.ftc.gov or 877-FTC-HELP to file a complaint against a debt collector or credit bureau; or for help with Internet, telemarketing, identity theft, or other fraud complaints. Use their extensive Web site for consumer information brochures, or to read copies of consumer protection laws.

National Credit Union Administration: This agency regulates credit unions. Visit www.ncua.gov or call 703-518-6300.

Office of Thrift Supervision: Handles complaints about federal savings and loans and federal savings banks. Visit www.ots.treas.gov or call 800-842-6929.

Kids and Money
Financial literacy is a vital skill for kids, but most learn through the school of hard knocks. Visit www.jumpstart.org to learn how you can help support financial literacy education. In addition, other resources are available at www.richdad.com.

Student Loan Consolidation
For information on how to consolidate your student loans and choose an affordable repayment plan visit www.SuccessDNA.com.

Web Sites
Following are some additional helpful Web sites. Since these may change, visit SuccessDNA.com for updates.

Call for Action is an international nonprofit network of consumer hotlines affiliated with local broadcast partners. Volunteer professionals assist consumers through mediation and education to help resolve problems with businesses and government agencies. Visit www.callforaction.org.

CardRatings.com: Provides free information on low-rate, secured, and other credit cards.

Circle Lending, Inc.: Borrow from (or lend to) friends and family for your small business or personal credit needs. Draft a free promissory note and loan proposal as well! Visit www.successdna.com for details.

Consumer Action: You'll get a free list of secured cards, a list of low-rate credit cards, and a variety of other helpful publications in many languages at www.consumer-action.org. (Please note, you must include the hyphen between the words "consumer" and "action" to get to the correct site.)

Consumer Federation of America: CFA lobbies for consumers' rights and also offers booklets on saving money, buying a home, managing debts, resolving consumer complaints, and so on. They're available online for free at: www.consumerfed.org.

ConsumerWorld.org is a very comprehensive site with lots of helpful consumer information, including credit, but also much more.

Credit.about.com offers helpful advice on reducing debt and solving credit issues.

Fraud.org: Home of the National Fraud Information Center, which gives consumers the information they need to avoid becoming victims of telemarketing and Internet fraud and to help them get their complaints to law enforcement agencies quickly and easily. If you suspect telemarketing or Internet fraud, visit their Web site immediately to file a complaint form.

About the Author

Garrett Sutton, Esq., author of *Own Your Own Corporation*, *The ABC's of Getting Out of Debt*, and *How to Buy and Sell a Business* (all included in the Rich Dad's Advisors® series), is an attorney with over twenty-five years of experience in assisting individuals and businesses to determine their appropriate corporate structure, limit their liability, protect their assets, and advance their financial, personal, and credit success goals.

Garrett and his law firm, Sutton Law Center, have offices in Reno, Nevada, Jackson Hole, Wyoming, and Sacramento, California. The firm represents hundreds of corporations, limited liability companies, limited partnerships, and individuals in their business-related law matters, including incorporations, contracts, and ongoing business-related legal advice. It continues to accept new clients.

Garrett attended Colorado College and the University of California at Berkeley, where he received a B.S. in business administration in 1975. He graduated with a J.D. in 1978 from Hastings College of Law, the University of California's law school in San Francisco. He has appeared in the *Wall Street Journal* and numerous other publications. He is the radio host of the nationally syndicated *Garrett Sutton Show*, which is archived at www.successdna.com.

Garrett is a member of the State Bar of Nevada, the State Bar of California, and the American Bar Association. He has written numerous professional articles and has served on the Publication Committee of the State Bar of Nevada.

Garrett enjoys speaking with entrepreneurs on the advantages of forming business entities. He is a frequent lecturer for the Small Business Administration and the Rich Dad's Advisors series.

Garrett serves on the boards of the American Baseball Foundation, located in Birmingham, Alabama, and the Reno-Nevada—based Sierra Kids Foundation.

For more information on Garrett Sutton and Sutton Law Center, please visit his website at www.sutlaw.com.

Where can I receive free credit success information?

For free credit resources, articles, and
other useful information, visit
www.successdna.com

How Can I Protect My Personal and Good Debt Assets?

For information on forming corporations, limited liability
companies, and limited partnerships to protect your
personal, real estate, and business holdings in all 50
states, as well as useful tips and strategies, visit
Altacian Corporate Services, Inc.'s Web site,
located at www.altacian.com
or call toll-free 1-800-785-9811.

ALTACIAN
CORPORATE
SERVICES

Where Can I Receive More Legal Information?

For free information on a variety of
legal topics, visit the Sutton Law
Center Web site at
www.sutlaw.com

SUTTON
LAW CENTER
A PROFESSIONAL CORPORATION

Robert Kiyosaki's Edumercial
An Educational Commercial

The Three Incomes

In the world of accounting, there are three different types of income: earned, passive, and portfolio. When my real dad said to me, "Go to school, get good grades, and find a safe secure job," he was recommending I work for earned income. When my rich dad said, "The rich don't work for money, they have their money work for them," he was talking about passive income and portfolio income. Passive income, in most cases, is derived from real estate investments. Portfolio income is income derived from paper assets, such as stocks, bonds, and mutual funds.

Rich Dad used to say, "The key to becoming wealthy is the ability to convert earned income into passive income and/or portfolio income as quickly as possible." He would say, "The taxes are highest on earned income. The least taxed income is passive income. That is another reason why you want your money working hard for you. The government taxes the income you work hard for—more than the income your money works hard for."

The Key to Financial Freedom

The key to financial freedom and great wealth is a person's ability or skill to convert earned income into passive income and/or portfolio income. That is the skill that my rich dad spent a lot of time teaching Mike and me. Having that skill is the reason my wife Kim and I are financially free, never needing to work again. We continue to work because we choose to. Today we own a real estate investment company for passive income and participate in private placements and initial public offerings of stock for portfolio income.

Investing to become rich requires a different set of personal skills – skills essential for financial success as well as low-risk and high-investment returns. In other words, knowing how to create assets that buy other assets. The problem is that gaining the basic education and experience required is often time consuming, frightening, and expensive, especially when you make mistakes with your own money. That is why I created the patented educational board games trademarked as CASHFLOW®.

The New York Times

writes:

"Move over, Monopoly®...
A new board game that
aims to teach people how
to get rich is gaining fans
the world over!"

MONOPOLY® is a trademark of Hasbro, Inc.

WHY PLAY GAMES?

Games are a **powerful learning tool**
because they enable
people to experience
"hands-on" learning.
As a **true reflection
of behavior**, games
are a **window to
our attitudes**, our
**abilities to see
opportunities**, and
**assess risk and
rewards.**

Each of the
CASHFLOW® games creates a
forum in which to evaluate life
decisions regarding money and
finances and immediately see the
results of your decisions.

**Play often and learn
what it takes to
*get out of the
Rat Race-*
for good!**

RichKidSmartKid.com

Money is a life skill—but we don't teach our children about money in school. I am asking for your help in getting financial education into the hands of interested teachers and school administrators.

RichKidSmartKid.com was created as an innovative and interactive Web site designed to convey key concepts about money and finance in ways that are fun and challenging…and educational for young people in grades K through 12. It contains 4 mini-games that teach:

Assets vs. Liabilities
Good Debt vs. Bad Debt
Importance of Charity
Passive Income vs. Earned Income

AND, schools may also register at www.richkidsmartkid.com to receive a FREE download of our electronic version of CASHFLOW for Kids at School.

How You Can Make a Difference

Play CASHFLOW for KIDs and CASHFLOW 101 with family and friends and share the richkidsmartkid.com Web site with your local teachers and school administrators.

Join me now in taking financial education to our schools and e-mail me of your interest at Iwill@richdad.com. Together we can better prepare our children for the financial world they will face.

Thank you!

DISCOVER THE POWER OF THESE RICH DAD PROGRAMS:

• Rich Dad's You Can Choose to Be Rich

• Rich Dad's 6 Steps to Becoming a Successful Real Estate Investor

• Rich Dad's How to Increase the Income from Your Real Estate Investments

Step-by-step guides with audio components and comprehensive workbooks ensure that you can take the knowledge you gain and apply it to increasing the value and profitability of your investment portfolio.

ARE YOU WINNING OR LOSING THE GAME OF MONEY?